CRANFORD

CRANFORD

by Elizabeth Gaskell

adapted for the stage by Laura Turner

JOSEF WEINBERGER PLAYS

LONDON

CRANFORD
First published in 2014
by Josef Weinberger Ltd
12-14 Mortimer Street, London W1T 3JJ
www.josef-weinberger.com / plays@jwmail.co.uk

ISBN: 978 0 85676 350 2

Printed by Commercial Colour Press plc, Hainault, Essex

To Mum and Dad, with love always

FOREWORD

My thanks and gratitude to everyone who helped and supported the development of this play: everyone at Chapterhouse both past and present; the cast and creative team behind the original production who worked so hard to bring Cranford to life, particularly Beck Gadsby for her enthusiasm, patience and support. To Richard Main at Chapterhouse, for giving me the chance to make Cranford real and asking all the right questions along the way, thank you so much.

To Matt Connell, Alex Cory and all at Berlin Associates, thank you.

To my mum, dad, nanna, friends, family and RWM, thank you for being there. Love to you all.

CRANFORD was first performed at Picton Castle, Pembrokeshire on 15th June 2011, presented by Chapterhouse Theatre Company. The cast was as follows:

MISS MATTY JENKYNS	Kirsty Cox
MISS POLE	Grace Miller
MRS JAMIESON	Jenni Lea-Jones
MARY SMITH	Kirsty Worthington
MISS JESSIE BROWN	Emily Swatton
MISS BROWN	Caroline Hallam
CAPTAIN BROWN	Stewart Barham
MAJOR GORDON	Ellis J Wells
MARTHA	Caroline Hallam
JEM HEARN	Adam Gayson
FANNY	Jenni Lea-Jones
MR MULLINER	Adam Grayson
THOMAS HOLBROOK	Stewart Barham
MRS BARKER	Jenni Lea-Jones
MRS FORRESTER	Caroline Hallam
SIGNOR BRUNONI	Ellis J Wells
FANNY'S SUITOR	Ellis J Wells
RAILWAY REPRESENTATIVE	Ellis J Wells
MILLINER	Caroline Hallam

Directed by Rebecca Gadsby

Set design by Peter Eldridge

Costumes designed by Georgina Nurse

CHARACTERS

Miss Matty Jenkyns

Miss Pole

Mrs Jamieson

Mary Smith

Miss Jessie Brown

Miss Brown (*Jessie's sister*)

Captain Brown (*Jessie's father*)

Major Gordon

Martha

Jem Hearn

Fanny

Mr Mulliner

Thomas Holbrook

Mrs Barker

Mrs Forrester

Signor Brunoni

Fanny's Suitor

Railway Representative

Milliner

Two Gentlemen

ACT ONE

Scene One

Exterior. Cranford Village. Day.

Enter MISS MATTY JENKYNS. *She is in her fifties and dressed in black mourning. Her movements are slow as she puts her purse down beside her and unties her bonnet. She opens her purse and draws out a St. Christopher's cross on a chain, looks at it and holds it close. She is suddenly overcome with grief. Enter* MARY SMITH. *She is in her twenties but has the air of someone older. She is also in black mourning. She hovers for a moment, then clears her throat.*

MISS MATTY *starts and rearranges her features immediately, wiping away tears and putting the chain around her neck.*

MISS MATTY Mary, my dear, there you are. What kept you? I think it's time we dye the curtain linings, don't you? They are quite shamefully faded.

MARY I don't think anyone will be looking at the lining of the –

MISS MATTY Every inch of a woman's house is liable to scrutiny.

(*She is struggling to fasten the chain around her neck.* MARY *fastens it for her.*)

MISS MATTY I shall send Fanny out with some money. Pink, I think. Don't you think pink?

(MARY *stops* MISS MATTY *as she tries to go inside her house.*)

MARY — Sit down for a moment. It's been a long day with much to contend with –

(MISS MATTY *turns to go again.*)

MARY — It would make me feel better if you were to stay a while.

(MISS MATTY *turns and goes back to* MARY.)

MARY — Grief is not weakness, Miss Matty.

MISS MATTY — I should like to be known as Matilda from now on. Deborah does not – did not like – "Matty". A vulgarisation, she said. I did many things she did not like during her lifetime, but no longer.

MARY — Matilda it is.

MISS MATTY — I must at least steam the kitchen broom. I've been asking Fanny to do it for days . . .

MARY — It is a terrible thing to lose a sister.

(MISS MATTY *stops, then her shoulders shake, which* MARY *mistakes for anger.*)

MARY — Miss Matty – Matilda – I did not mean to . . . I'm sorry, I shall not mention it again –

(MISS MATTY *turns and* MARY *sees she is crying. They embrace.*)

MISS POLE — (*from offstage*) Miss Matty! Miss Matty!

(*Enter* MISS POLE. *She is breathless with excitement.*)

MISS POLE — Good heavens! What's wrong? I have news that shall divert you, Miss Matty –

(MISS POLE *breaks off as* MARY *whispers in her ear.*)

MISS POLE — Matilda? Why on earth should I call her that? Now, I have some most grievous news.

MARY — Must you tell us now if it is so very bad?

(MARY *tries to subtly nod her head towards* MISS MATTY *several times.*)

MISS POLE — Do you have a neck ache, my dear? Now, it came about just as I was leaving Mrs Forrester's house and I happened to glance up towards the village and what did I see? You will not believe it – in fact, I can hardly bring myself to say it.

MARY — Then say it quickly and be done with it!

MISS POLE — It was – a man!

(*Exclamations of horror.*)

MISS MATTY — It can't be!

MARY — Are you sure?

MISS POLE — A man! As bold as brass!

MARY — He must be visiting. Doesn't Mrs Forrester have a male relative?

MISS POLE — The coach was piled high, not only with luggage but with furniture! I deduce he is to – take lodgings here!

MARY — But what would he do here?

MISS MATTY — (*in agreement with* MARY) The surgeon has his round and has to sleep here, but not every man may be a surgeon!

MISS POLE — There is more. If it was not bad enough we have been invaded by a man – he is a gentleman! He wears military dress!

(*From offstage, the sound of a hunting horn. Enter* MR MULLINER, *blowing the horn. He is a tall, snotty-faced man, wearing a butler outfit.*)

MR MULLINER — The Honourable Mrs Jamieson.

(*Enter* MRS JAMIESON. *She is dressed lavishly and in her arms holds her dog, Carlo.*)

MRS JAMIESON — Ladies, I have intelligence –

(MARY *goes to stroke Carlo, but withdraws when the dog tries to bite her.*)

MARY — Miss Pole has already told us! A man! In the village!

MRS JAMIESON — But you do not know, I presume, that he is walking up the street towards your house at this very moment?

MISS POLE — (*flustered*) Quickly! Within! We must not been seen standing around in the street like Stonehenge!

(*Exeunt* MISS POLE, MISS MATTY, MARY *and* MRS JAMIESON. *The window of* MISS MATTY*'s house slowly opens.* MISS POLE *peers out to ascertain the coast is clear. The heads* *of* MISS MATTY, MRS JAMIESON *and* MARY *appear in the window, jostling for a good view.*)

MRS JAMIESON (*in annoyance, to* MR MULLINER) Mr Mulliner! Don't just stand there! You will alert the man to our presence

(*Exit* MR MULLINER.)

MISS MATTY I do not see him!

MISS POLE Mary, move over, my dear!

MARY There! There he is!

(*The other women crane to see where* MARY *points. Enter* CAPTAIN BROWN, *followed by his daughters,* JESSIE *and* MISS BROWN. CAPTAIN BROWN *cuts a striking figure in his military outfit but* MISS BROWN *is sickly and struggles to walk, even with* JESSIE'S *assistance.*)

MISS MATTY He really is coming this way!

MISS POLE And he brings two wives with him!

MISS MATTY (*sotto*) They cannot be his wives; they are far too young!

MRS JAMIESON They are young. They are certainly his wives.

(CAPTAIN BROWN *looks up, perhaps having heard their mutters, and sees the women.*)

CAPT. BROWN Good day, ladies!

(*The women freeze in horror. Collecting herself first,* MISS MATTY *gives a regal wave. The other women copy her.* CAPTAIN BROWN *returns the wave and continues on his way.*)

MISS MATTY It is worse than we thought.

MISS POLE He clearly has no regard for common forms of courtesy! Imagining bidding us good day!

MISS MATTY That was over-familiar indeed.

(*Exeunt* CAPTAIN, JESSIE *and* MARY BROWN.)

MARY They are out of sight.

(MISS POLE *shuts the window. Enter* MISS POLE, MRS JAMIESON, MISS MATTY *and* MISS BROWN, *followed by an unenthusiastic* MR MULLINER. MARY *rushes to the wall to watch* CAPTAIN BROWN'S *progress.*)

MARY They are going into a house! They are to be our neighbours!

MRS JAMIESON I feel sorry for those two young ladies. A man is always so in the way in the house, isn't he, Carlo?

MISS POLE They do not have my sympathy! What are we to do about this?

MARY What is there to do about it?

MISS MATTY Nothing. We shall wait until we meet the gentleman in question.

MRS JAMIESON Meet him? I certainly hope we will not encounter him in the ladies' parlours of Cranford! Mr Mulliner, the sedan.

MR MULLINER Yes, my lady.

(*Exeunt* MR MULLINER, *followed by* MRS JAMIESON, *fussing over Carlo.*)

MISS POLE (*to* MARY) My cousin has sent me some new knitting patterns. (*In excitement.*) For summer petticoats!

MARY I think I should perhaps stay here.

MISS POLE (*to* MISS MATTY) Oh, she is all right, aren't you, dear?

(*Exeunt* MISS POLE *and a resisting* MARY.)

MISS MATTY (*to the absent Deborah*) You always said you would not live to see the day a man moved to Cranford.

(*Exit* MISS MATTY.)

Scene Two

Exterior. Cranford Village Green. Day.

Enter MISS MATTY, MARY, MISS POLE *and* MRS JAMIESON, *followed by* MR MULLINER. MRS JAMIESON *carries Carlo the dog in her arms.*

MRS JAMIESON (*to Carlo*) There, there, my precious, there, there. (*To the women.*) What is the delay? It is growing most tiresome. There is a most incommodious breeze around the ankles. (*To* MR MULLINER.) Take poor Carlo home.

(*She hands Carlo to an unimpressed* Mr Mulliner. *To the women.*) He simply cannot wait beyond four for his tea, he gets so cranky when he's hungry –

(*Enter a* Railway Representative, *silencing* Mrs Jamieson. *He is breathless and holds a briefcase.*)

Miss Matty (*to the* Man) Are you the representative from the railway company, sir?

Railway Rep. Forgive my tardiness. I am so pleased you were all able to make it here today to discuss the imminent arrival of the Cranford rail line –

Mrs Jamieson I think you have quite mistaken our intentions.

Miss Pole We are here to dispute not to celebrate the railroad!

Miss Matty What Miss Pole means to say is we are yet to be convinced of the advantages of connecting this rural village, where we live a most confined and contented existence, to the . . . (*As diplomatically as she can.*) alternative attractions . . . of the metropolis.

Railway Rep. Do your husbands concur with these complaints?

Miss Matty I think you will find, sir, that all the holders of houses above a certain rent are women.

Miss Pole There are no men to be attended upon here.

Capt. Brown (*offstage*) Good day there!

(*Enter* CAPTAIN, *helping* JESSIE *and* MISS BROWN.)

RAILWAY REP. Captain Brown!

(*To the women's surprise, the* RAILWAY REPRESENTATIVE *steps forward to shake* CAPTAIN BROWN'S *hand.*)

CAPT. BROWN One moment, sir!

(CAPTAIN BROWN *helps his daughters.*)

MISS POLE (*sotto*) That was most disrespectful.

MARY (*sotto*) It is admirable that he helps his daughter. She looks so unwell.

(MISS BROWN *leans heavily on* JESSIE, *coughing into her handkerchief from exertion.* CAPTAIN BROWN *shakes hands jovially with the* RAILWAY REP.)

CAPT. BROWN Now, what is all this?

MISS POLE A meeting in disagreement of the obnoxious railroad.

CAPT. BROWN Then I am loath to reveal my identity.

MISS MATTY What do you mean, sir?

CAPT. BROWN When I retired my position, I was fortunate to find employment with a railway company. I was despatched here with my daughters, Jessie and Mary, to supervise the new rail line. But I anticipate now this may not serve me well in your eyes.

(MISS BROWN *suddenly collapses a little more against her sister, coughing.* JESSIE *struggles to support her. The coughing agitates Carlo in* MR MULLINER'S *arms next to* MISS BROWN. MRS JAMIESON *and* CAPTAIN BROWN *rush towards Carlo /* MISS BROWN.)

MRS JAMIESON Carlo, baby, come to mama!

CAPT. BROWN (*sidestepping* MRS JAMIESON *to try and get to* MISS BROWN) Excuse me!

JESSIE (*in alarm*) Father!

(JESSIE *is unable to support* MISS BROWN *any longer and she falls heavily against* MR MULLINER, *who is trying to pass Carlo to* MRS JAMIESON. MR MULLINER *and Carlo both go flying, to* MRS JAMIESON'S *horror.*

MRS JAMIESON *dives into the melee as* CAPTAIN BROWN *lifts* MISS BROWN *in his arms.* MRS JAMIESON *rescues Carlo as* MARY *and* MISS MATTY *help* MR MULLINER *up.*)

MRS JAMIESON (*to Carlo*) It's alright, my precious! Mama's here! Carlo, speak to me! (*She leans her head close to Carlo.*) He is injured! Quickly, we must summon the surgeon!

MISS POLE Come, my house is nearest! The doctor may attend you there!

(*Exeunt* MISS POLE, MRS JAMIESON *with Carlo and* MR MULLINER.)

CAPT. BROWN (*to the remaining ladies*) I must attend to my daughter.

(*Exeunt* CAPTAIN, MISS BROWN *and* JESSIE BROWN.)

RAILWAY REP. Will you take some literature, ladies? Perhaps if you learn a little more of the benefits of the railroad . . .

(*He holds out some leaflets.*)

MISS MATTY We have a philosophy here in Cranford. We quite despise the modern idea of women being equal to men. They are superior in every way. Good day.

(*Exeunt* MISS MATTY *and* MARY. *Exit the* RAILWAY REP, *the other way.*)

Scene Three

Exterior. The garden at MISS MATTY'S. *Day.*

Enter FANNY, MISS MATTY'S *maid. She arranges the garden furniture.* FANNY'S SUITOR *peeps over the wall. He wolf-whistles at* FANNY, *then ducks out of sight.* FANNY *goes back to her work.* FANNY'S SUITOR *jumps over the wall, then creeps up behind* FANNY *and grabs her, making her jump.*

FANNY Gah, worra yer doin? If ma mistress catches yer here, yer'll be forrit!

SUITOR Eyh, that anyway to tret yer fella?

FANNY Depend if yer my fella or not, wunt it? I heard yer's been getting up ter all sorts with that Miss Pole's Jenny!

SUITOR I'll show yer what I think of Miss Pole's Jenny.

(*He kisses* FANNY. *She allows it for a minute.*)

FANNY Gerra way. Miss Matty'll be out in a minute and I'll be forrit and all!

(*He starts to slope off.*)

FANNY Oi! Come ter kitchen door later. There'll be lunch leftovers.

SUITOR That all?

FANNY (*suggestively*) Have ter see, wunt yer?

(*Exit* SUITOR. FANNY *finishes arranging the chairs. Enter* MISS MATTY, MISS POLE *and* MARY.)

MISS MATTY Fanny, have you put the kettle on yet?

FANNY No, ma'am.

MISS MATTY Then do not delay! Tea must be ready to serve in case we receive callers this afternoon. And I should like you to clean the tops of the bookcases.

FANNY Nobody canna see dust on the top!

MISS MATTY But I know it is there, and I should rather know it is not.

FANNY I canna reach!

MISS MATTY Then you may stand on a chair.

FANNY Yes, ma'am.

MISS MATTY — And who was that gentleman I saw outside the gate just now?

FANNY — Gentleman?

MISS MATTY — You know you are not permitted followers.

FANNY — Please, ma'am, I never have more than one at a time.

(FANNY *takes a chair.*)

MISS MATTY — I meant one from the kitchen!

(*Exit* FANNY.)

MISS POLE — (*watching her go*) That is the gait of a girl who entertains far too many flirtations.

MISS MATTY — It is a constant anxiety to me.

(*From within the house, an almighty crash and a screech.*)

MISS POLE — There is nothing for it; she shall have to go.

MISS MATTY — Mary, would you pen an advertisement for a replacement?

(*Enter* FANNY, *holding the broken leg of the chair.*)

MISS MATTY — Tell me that isn't my garden chair.

FANNY — I could tell yer, ma'am, but I'd be lyin'. It weren't my fault!

MISS MATTY — Mary, could you also send word to the joiners. We shall be requiring their services. That is all, Fanny.

FANNY — There's a lady in the parlour, ma'am.

(*The women react with shock.*)

MISS MATTY — What could she want at this time of day? Calling hours have not yet commenced!

FANNY — Shall I bring her out, ma'am?

MISS MATTY — No! I am still in my morning dress! I must change my hat at least. Fanny, fetch the calling caps!

(*Exit* FANNY. *The women hurry to arrange themselves.* MARY *and* MISS MATTY *untie each other's caps.*)

MARY — Maybe something out of the ordinary has happened.

MISS POLE — Nothing short of a death in the family should warrant such blatant disregard for social etiquette! (*She realizes what she has said. To* MISS MATTY.) Sorry, dear.

(*Enter* FANNY, *holding two bonnets. She gives one each to* MISS MATTY *and* MARY *and takes their caps in return. They put the bonnets on.*)

MISS MATTY — Very well, show her out.

(*Exit* FANNY.)

MISS POLE — Make some conversation, Miss Smith, or we shall look like we have nothing better to do than wait for callers!

MARY — The . . . grass is very attractive at this time of year.

(*Enter* JESSIE BROWN.)

JESSIE Good day. Miss Jenkyns, I believe? I hope you will forgive me, but I so wanted to introduce myself to you properly now we are neighbours.

MISS POLE But it is only the second day.

JESSIE I'm sorry?

MISS MATTY Miss Brown, sit down. It is clear to me that you have been in the way of remaining indoors with your sister for a long time.

JESSIE (*in agreement*) She has been unwell for many years now.

MISS MATTY Then there are some things that you must learn, Miss Brown.

JESSIE Please, call me Jessie.

MISS POLE (*unable to contain herself*) Not until the third week of our acquaintance!

MARY (*seeing* JESSIE'S *confusion*) Amongst us ladies, I am now known as Mary, but when I first arrived I was only Miss Smith. And I still go as such when in polite society.

MISS POLE Not that our society is not polite! But accepted forms of address are relaxed when we are alone together. I am Miss Pole.

(JESSIE *shakes her hand.*)

JESSIE In time, may I know you by another name, Miss Pole?

(Miss Pole *looks away, horrified.*)

Mary (*sotto*) Miss Pole prefers to be known only as Miss Pole.

Miss Matty But within three weeks I shall be Miss Matilda to you.

Jessie I'm afraid I am quite unused to the ways of the world.

Miss Matty These are not the ways of the world. These are the ways of Cranford.

Miss Pole Calling hours are from twelve until three.

Jessie (*realizing her error in calling so early*) Oh . . .

Miss Matty (*kindly*) We shall forgive the oversight on this occasion. You are new.

Jessie Miss Pole – if I may be so bold – how come you to be visiting outside the allocated period?

Miss Pole (*affronted*) I am a close acquaintance!

Mary We are entitled to – adjust the rules – if it is seen fit.

Miss Pole But never must more than three days elapse between receiving a call and returning it.

Mary And never stay longer than a quarter of an hour.

Jessie Am I to look at my watch? How am I to find out when a quarter of an hour has passed?

MISS MATTY You must keep thinking about the time and not allow yourself to forget it in conversation.

JESSIE What if you become immersed in some absorbing subject?

MISS POLE During calling hours? That would not do at all.

MISS MATTY If you hold a dinner –

MISS POLE (*interrupting*) – which, given your sister's sickly state, you are most unadvised to do.

MISS MATTY (*continuing*) It is most vulgar to give anything expensive to eat or drink.

MISS POLE The Honourable Mrs Jamieson gives bread and butter and she is sister-in-law to the Earl of Glenmire.

MARY Money-spending is regarded as quite vulgar and ostentatious.

MISS MATTY Elegant Economy. That is what we practise here, Miss Brown.

MISS POLE Always dress with chaste elegance and propriety.

(JESSIE *adjusts her skirt self-consciously.*)

MISS MATTY And recall that the inhabitants of Cranford keep early hours. The whole town is abed and asleep by half-past ten. Evening gatherings should never be prolonged beyond nine o'clock.

(MISS POLE *catches sight of her watch in horror.*)

MISS POLE Miss Matty!

(MISS POLE *thrusts her watch in* MISS MATTY'S *face.* MISS MATTY *reacts with shock, but calms her features. She stands, followed by* MISS POLE.)

MISS MATTY Do send our best wishes to your sister and father, Miss Brown. If she suffers regularly from a cough, I suggest cider vinegar mixed with honey, twice a day.

(MISS POLE *tugs on* MARY'S *arm until she stands.* JESSIE *realizes she should leave and stands awkwardly.*)

JESSIE Thank you. Perhaps you would join us for tea – during calling hours on the fourth day – to thank you for your hospitality –

MISS MATTY That would not do at all. It is far too soon for you to be making invitations. You must come here. We will take tea in the garden, given the clement weather.

JESSIE My father shall be delighted. Good day!

(*Exit* JESSIE.)

MISS POLE Did you mean to invite him?

MISS MATTY I do not think it matters whether I meant to or not as it seems he will be attending.

MISS POLE Do you know, I think it is time for Miss Jessie Brown to leave off her dimples and not try to look like a child.

MARY — I found her quite charming.

MISS POLE — It would not have been half so charming if she had lingered here until calling hours began. It is almost twelve! Imagine if she were seen wandering about by Mrs Jamieson!

MISS MATTY — Quite. And we must retire inside before Mrs Jamieson finds us browning ourselves in the garden.

(*Exeunt.*)

Scene Four

Exterior. Cranford Village. Day.

The window of MISS POLE'S *house opens.* MISS POLE'S *head peers out.*

MISS POLE — (*sotto*) Miss Matty! (*Slightly louder.*) Miss Matty!

(*The window of* MISS MATTY'S *house opens.* MISS MATTY'S *head appears.*)

MISS POLE — Do you have any flour? I am making scones and find myself quite adrift!

MISS MATTY — I shall ask Fanny to fetch some from the pantry. The cheek I have had from that girl today! I will be relieved when the new girl arrives.

(*Enter* MAJOR GORDON, *walking briskly.* MISS POLE *sees him.*)

MISS POLE — (*in horror*) I cannot believe it Another one!

Miss Matty Another what?

Miss Pole Lower your voice, my dear, withdraw calmly and quickly from the window and bolt it tightly!

Maj. Gordon (*to* Miss Matty*, having spotted her*) Good day there!

(Miss Pole *freezes.*)

Maj. Gordon (*to* Miss Pole) And good day to you, madam!

(Miss Pole *looks away, her face frozen in shock.*)

Miss Matty Good day, sir.

Maj. Gordon I wonder if you might help me – I'm looking for the – (*He consults a paper.*) Lamb and Flag at Cranford?

Miss Matty Continue on to the village green and you will see the establishment. Are you to stay long, sir?

Maj. Gordon I am visiting a friend who has recently taken lodgings here. A Captain Brown?

Miss Matty (*slightly disapprovingly*) We have met.

Maj. Gordon (*not sensing the tone*) Excellent! Perhaps we shall meet again soon then if we keep the same society.

(Major Gordon *goes to continue on his way.*)

Miss Pole (*unable to contain herself*) Miss Matty is to host a garden party tomorrow afternoon!

MAJ. GORDON (*in surprised confusion*) How pleasant.

(MISS POLE *turns away as* MISS MATTY *glares at her.*)

MISS MATTY You must join us at three tomorrow, Mr . . .

MAJ. GORDON Major Gordon. I should be delighted. Good day!

(*Exit* MAJOR GORDON.)

MISS POLE I can see from your expression, Matty dear, that you agree it was most insidious of him to garner an invitation for himself to your garden party. And imagine conversing with someone through their window! The very idea!

(MISS MATTY *and* MISS POLE *disappear inside their houses, pulling the windows closed.*)

Scene Five

Exterior. The garden at MISS MATTY'S. *Day.*

Enter FANNY *with a basket of washing, followed by* MARTHA *who is struggling with the heavy washing tub.* FANNY *separates white washing, giving it to* MARTHA *to put in the tub.*

FANNY Mornings is breakfast, then chores round the house. Dusting, cleaning, making the beds, but if there's baking ter do, yer best ter do it before callin' hours.

(JEM HEARN *appears at the gate. He watches* MARTHA *with interest until she glances back and sees him. She ignores him.*)

FANNY Afternoons is washin' and tidyin', but if yer runnin shorta time, just open a window and hang up some lavender, Miss Matty never notices the difference. (*She passes a dark sheet to* MARTHA.) Keep holda this one a minute.

(*Distracted as she glances over at* JEM, MARTHA *puts the sheet straight into the tub with the others.* FANNY *notices.*)

FANNY Oi, watch it! Yer'll send the whites grey.

(MARTHA *takes up the dark sheet and looks over her shoulder, annoyed to see* JEM *still looking.*)

MARTHA (*in annoyance*) Watchya lookin' at?

(FANNY *sees* JEM.)

FANNY Worra you doin here, Jem Hearn?

(JEM *holds up his bag of tools.*)

JEM Broken chair, ain't it?

FANNY S'pose yer better come in then.

(JEM *comes through the gate.*)

FANNY (*flirtaciously*) Ain't seen yer bout much.

JEM (*to* MARTHA) Ain't seen yer round before.

FANNY She's new.

JEM (*to* MARTHA) Got a name?

MARTHA Mind yer own!

FANNY (*annoyed*) Yer better go in then.

JEM (*to* MARTHA) See yer later, mind-yer-own.

MARTHA (*to* JEM, *harshly*) Not if I see yer first, nosey parker!

(*Exit* JEM.)

FANNY Yer not allowed followers.

MARTHA Pass the sheets, then.

FANNY Yer'll lose yer position if yer go entertainin'.

(MARTHA *starts doing* FANNY'S *job separating the whites.*)

FANNY That Jem Hearn's gorra right proper reputation round here.

(*The window of* MISS MATTY'S *house flies open and* MISS MATTY'S *head appears.*)

MISS MATTY Fanny, Martha, what are you still doing out here? The guests will be here any moment. Inside with you and get the teas ready to serve!

(*The window closes.* MARTHA *grabs the basket of dark washing.*)

MARTHA Bring the whites in then!

(*Exit* MARTHA. *Furious,* FANNY *goes to pick up the tub of whites but pauses as she sees the dark sheets she is still holding. She quickly stuffs a dark sheet amongst the whites and picks up the tub. Exit* FANNY. *Enter* MISS POLE, MISS MATTY *and* MARY.)

MISS POLE — I hope that new maid of yours shan't embarrass you this afternoon, Matty. She does know how to serve tea, doesn't she?

(MISS MATTY *and* MARY *hold bottles containing varying amounts of lemonade, which they decant into one carafe, as* MISS POLE *arranges the garden chairs around the table.*)

MARY — She has settled in rather well. There has only been one incident involving a scrubbing brush and a stray mouse.

(*Enter* FANNY, CAPTAIN *and* JESSIE BROWN.)

FANNY — Captain and Miss Brown, ma'am.

(*Exit* FANNY.)

MARY — Miss Brown, where is your sister?

JESSIE — I'm afraid she was not well enough for company this afternoon.

MISS MATTY — It seems she suffers very greatly.

CAPT. BROWN — (*fondly*) Jessie does all she can to alleviate poor Mary's distress.

(*Enter* MARTHA *with a tray of tea, which wobbles violently in her hands. She reaches the table and thumps the tray down gratefully.*)

MARTHA — Are all yer guests come, ma'am? Shall I shut up the garden gate?

MISS MATTY — We are still expecting Mrs Barker.

(MARTHA *turns to go.*)

MISS MATTY — The tea, Martha?

(MARTHA *turns back, a look of horror on her face.*)

MISS MATTY — (*to* CAPTAIN BROWN *and* JESSIE, *by way of explanation*) Mrs Barker is a widow and therefore permitted some laxity in the normal confines of time-keeping.

(MARTHA *hands round cups clumsily. She picks up the teapot, and sloshes tea near* CAPTAIN BROWN'S *lap.*)

MISS MATTY — Martha!

MARTHA — Beggin' yer pardon, sir!

(MARTHA *goes to dab at* CAPTAIN BROWN'S *trousers with her apron.*)

MISS POLE — Desist, girl!

(MARTHA *steps away, shame-faced.*)

CAPT. BROWN — (*kindly*) Quite all right! No damage done at all! Now, I must insist you allow me to pour the tea, my dear. This pot is far too heavy for a lady.

(MISS POLE *frowns as* CAPTAIN BROWN *pours tea.*)

MISS MATTY Martha, the sponge wafers please.

(MARTHA *looks terrified.* MARY *takes* MARTHA *aside.*)

MARY Take the wafers around, and let people help themselves. And go first to the ladies. Always go to ladies before gentlemen when you are waiting.

MARTHA (*bemused*) I'll do it as you tell me, ma'am, but I like lads best.

(MARTHA *offers round a plate. Enter* JEM HEARN. *He doesn't have his bag. He watches* MARTHA *appreciatively, then notices* MARY *looking at him.*)

JEM Yer chair's all fixed up, ma'am.

MARY Thank you. Have your master send us the bill.

(JEM *turns to go, but glances back at* MARTHA. MARY *notices. Exit* JEM. *Enter* MRS BARKER, *in floods of tears.*)

MISS POLE My dear Mrs Barker! What on earth is wrong?

MRS BARKER Oh, it is too much!

MISS POLE What has happened?

MRS BARKER It's Bessie! She has fallen into the lime pit!

JESSIE (*in horror*) Her daughter?

MISS POLE Her cow! (*Sotto.*) Although she looks upon it quite as a daughter. (*To* MRS BARKER.) We must raise the alarm, my dear, and have her removed immediately!

MRS BARKER She has been rescued. She was heard crying, the poor baby, and drawn straight out but – oh!

(MRS BARKER *descends into sobs.*)

MISS POLE She is not deformed in some way?

(MRS BARKER *cries louder.*)

MISS MATTY Quickly, my dear, tell us the worst.

MRS BARKER Oh, she went into the pit quite the beautiful, intelligent creature she always was, but when she came out, she was – oh, she is – quite bald!

(*The women share* MRS BARKER'S *horror.*)

MARY Not all over?

MRS BARKER All over! She is quite naked! It is shameful!

MISS POLE Have you tried a bath of oil?

MISS MATTY Applied chopped lettuce?

MARY Used a soft brush to stimulate hair growth?

MRS BARKER (*nodding*) All to no avail!

CAPT. BROWN Get her a flannel waistcoat and flannel drawers, ma'am, if you wish to keep her alive.

MRS BARKER (*in surprise*) Flannel?

CAPT. BROWN Flannel.

MRS BARKER I believe I have a roll at home that may do!

JESSIE How delightful! You never see cows dressed in flannel in London!

MRS BARKER Matty, forgive me, I must search out a pattern. Do you think Bessie will fit a plus size bloomer?

(*Exit* MRS BARKER *in excitement.*)

MARY Captain Brown, that was an ingenious idea!

CAPT. BROWN It is Jessie here who should take the thanks. The notion was prompted by the memory of her younger self singing to as she cut out and stitched underclothes for her dolls, lest they freeze in their nakedness!

MARY Miss Brown, you sing!

JESSIE It was a youthful inclination, nothing more.

CAPT. BROWN My daughter is too modest. She is most accomplished. (*To* JESSIE.) Give us a verse or two!

JESSIE (*to* MISS MATTY, *nervously*) Would that be appropriate?

MISS MATTY I think given the time of day and the natural lull in conversation, it would be fitting.

(JESSIE *stands and sings, prettily. Enter* MAJOR GORDON, *while she is singing. He watches* JESSIE *in admiration.* JESSIE *looks around and spots* MAJOR GORDON. *She falters and stops. The rest of the party follow her eyeline and see* MAJOR GORDON. JESSIE *completes her song.* MAJOR GORDON *is the first to applaud.* CAPTAIN BROWN *approaches* MAJOR GORDON *and shakes his hand warmly.*)

CAPT. BROWN Good lord, Gordon! What are you doing here?

MAJ. GORDON I'm on leave and thought I should like nothing better than to see my old friend Brown and his daughters again. Your neighbour was kind enough to invite me. (*To* JESSIE.) I trust you are well, Miss Brown?

JESSIE Very well, thank you.

MAJ. GORDON And your sister? Is she improved?

JESSIE Sadly not, sir.

MAJ. GORDON That is grievous news indeed.

(MAJOR GORDON *offers* JESSIE *his arm, which she takes. They walk a little way off, immediately deep in conversation.*)

MISS POLE (*to* CAPTAIN BROWN) Are we to expect a match?

CAPT. BROWN It has long been my desire. But I fear Jessie is not of a matrimonial mind. She is so consumed with her sister.

MISS POLE In that case, I should like to know precisely what good you see in the railway, Captain.

CAPT. BROWN What good?

MISS MATTY Evidently you must see some, or you would not have taken a job with the company.

CAPT. BROWN I'm afraid the good I saw in it was a living for myself and my daughters!

MISS POLE Excuse me?

CAPT. BROWN We should be quite destitute without this source of income. I am a man of modest means.

MISS MATTY Captain Brown, do not speak of money. It is a subject that savours of commerce and trade and we at Cranford have nothing to do with that.

CAPT. BROWN But I have no qualm with discussing my poverty.

MISS POLE If you must speak of it, whisper it indoors to an intimate friend only!

CAPT. BROWN Being poor is no disgrace.

MISS POLE Then tell me, Captain Brown, what do you consider a disgrace?

CAPT. BROWN Not this spread, for certain! I thank you, Miss Jenkyns.

(*Enter* FANNY *and* MARTHA. MARTHA *looks distraught and is holding a broken coal shovel.*)

FANNY There's been an accident with the coal shovel, ma'am.

MISS MATTY What on earth happened?

FANNY I just walked in and found her with it like that, ma'am. I gave her a smack, ma'am!

(MARTHA *starts crying.*)

MISS MATTY (*to* MARTHA) Dry your tears. Go inside and finish the dusting.

(*Exit* MARTHA.)

MISS MATTY (*to* FANNY) Don't leave her unattended again.

FANNY It weren't my fault! I canna stop her from being a daft oaf!

MISS POLE Do not speak to your mistress like that! (*To* MISS MATTY.) Send the girl to bed without supper!

MISS MATTY Yes, no supper tonight, Fanny.

(*Exit* FANNY, *angrily.* MISS MATTY *looks at the shovel sadly.*)

MISS MATTY The grating of the iron always used to annoy my sister so. I think she quite wished for a wooden one.

CAPT. BROWN Perhaps it is time we retire. Thank you again for your kind hospitality. Gordon, Mary would be most pleased to see you.

(*Exeunt* MAJOR GORDON, CAPTAIN BROWN *and* JESSIE.)

MISS POLE Can you believe he spoke of money in public? And in such a loud voice!

MISS MATTY Quite. Send him to Coventry, I say!

(*Exeunt.*)

Scene Six

Exterior. Cranford Village. Day.

Enter FANNY, *carrying her case. Enter* MARTHA, *looking desperate.*

MARTHA Where yer goin'? Come back!

FANNY I've had enough of bein' tret like a slave. Yer wanted the job!

MARTHA But I don't know how to make a pudding yet!

(*Exit* FANNY. MARTHA *collapses into tears.* JEM HEARN *appears at the gate. He sees* MARTHA *crying.*)

JEM Yer all right?

MARTHA Don't go sneakin' up on a gal like that! What yer doin' back here?

JEM Forgot me bag, didn't I?

MARTHA Sure you didn't leave it behind on purpose?

JEM Why would I do a thing like that?

(JEM *smiles at her but* MARTHA *goes to leave.*)

JEM Canna come in then? Ter get my bag?

MARTHA Yer'll have ter wait here. I'm in enough trouble as it is and I'll be turned out if my mistress sees yer here! She'll think yer my follower!

JEM Wouldn't be that bad, would it?

(MARTHA *storms over to him angrily.*)

MARTHA I need my position! I've gorra father laid up at home dependin' on me and my wage. But what would yer know about that with yer fancy carpenter lifestyle?

(MARTHA *bursts into tears and turns away.* JEM *hovers awkwardly for a moment, then puts a hand on her shoulder. She shrugs him off and turns on him, vicious.*)

MARTHA Don't think I'm one of them lasses yer can give a smile ter and then have yer wicked way with!

(JEM *can't stop himself from laughing at her.* MARTHA *turns on him. He backs away as she advances.*)

MARTHA (*furiously*) Yer laughin' at me?

JEM (*through his laughter*) No.

MARTHA Yer think it's funny do yer, getting' young gals sent out of work?

MISS MATTY (*offstage, angrily*) Martha!

(*Panicked,* MARTHA *shoves* JEM. *He topples backwards over the wall. Enter* MISS MATTY *holding grey sheets.*)

MISS MATTY Do my eyes deceive me, or are my white bed linens suddenly transformed to grey?

MARTHA: I dint . . . I made sure . . . please don't send me out! I'll do better, I promise!

MISS MATTY: Come inside. I hope your hands are hard-wearing. You'll be at the bleach all afternoon.

(*Exeunt.* JEM *peers over the wall. He sees the coast is clear and gets up. The window of* MISS MATTY'S *opens. His bag is dropped out. He goes over to pick it up and sees* MARTHA *in the window. She slams the window closed. Exit* JEM.)

ACT TWO

Scene One

Exterior. Cranford Village. Day.

Enter MARY *and* JESSIE, *walking arm in arm.*

MARY — So you have known him many years.

JESSIE — Major Gordon has been close to my father for several years.

MARY — Yes, but what is there between you?

JESSIE — Nothing.

(MARY *looks disbelieving.*)

JESSIE — Nothing!

(*Enter* MAJOR GORDON *with a crate.*)

MARY — Perhaps I shall ask him for myself. Good day, Major Gordon!

MAJ. GORDON — Ladies, I was just on my way to disseminate a gift.

(MAJOR GORDON *reveals the contents of the crate – oranges. The women gasp in delight.*)

MAJ. GORDON — A shipment just came into Manchester before I left.

MARY — They are Miss Matty's favourite! The deliveries hardly ever make it this far into the country.

MAJ. GORDON That will all change when the railroad arrives; that must be one benefit at least! But you must take as many as you like.

(MARY *takes some oranges.*)

MARY I shall take them to her now; thank you.

(JESSIE *grabs her sleeve tightly to try and prevent her leaving.* MARY *tugs herself free. Exit* MARY.)

MAJ. GORDON Won't you take an orange, Miss Brown?

(JESSIE *takes an orange.*)

MAJ. GORDON And please, some for your sister and father.

(JESSIE *takes a couple more, but accidentally drops all three. They scatter everywhere.* MAJOR GORDON *puts down his crate to help pick them up – their hands touch as they both reach for the last orange. They freeze and their eyes meet.* JESSIE *pulls away first and stands at a respectable distance.* MAJOR GORDON *gives her the orange.*)

MAJ. GORDON (*in a rush*) Miss Brown, would you like to . . . may I be so bold as to ask if you might . . . sit with me for a moment?

(*They sit together and talk quietly. Behind them, the window of* MISS MATTY'S *house opens.* MISS POLE'S *head appears. She looks surprised to see* JESSIE *and* MAJOR GORDON. *As she watches,* MAJOR GORDON *puts his arm behind* JESSIE *and eventually creeps it around her waist.*)

MISS POLE (*sotto*) Miss Matty! Miss Matty, there is a gentleman with his arm around Miss Jessie Brown's waist!

(MISS MATTY *appears at the window.*)

MISS MATTY The most proper place in the world for his arm to be. Come and eat your orange.

(MISS MATTY *pulls a resisting* MISS POLE *inside and closes the window.*)

MAJ. GORDON Perhaps we may meet again tomorrow. We might talk more of the future.

(JESSIE *smiles but suddenly turns away.*)

JESSIE I cannot. I must look after my sister.

MAJ. GORDON But surely your father will afford you a few hours' leisure?

JESSIE I'm sorry. I cannot. I'm sorry.

(*Exit* JESSIE.)

MAJ. GORDON Miss Brown!

(MAJOR GORDON *grabs his crate and follows her. Exit* MAJOR GORDON.)

Scene Two

Exterior. The garden at MISS MATTY'S. *Day.*

Enter MARTHA, *who arranges the garden chairs. Enter* MISS POLE *and* MARY, *holding their oranges.*

MISS POLE Oranges are such a curious proceeding.

(Mary *gives her a confused look.*)

Miss Pole (*lowering her voice*) The elder Miss Jenkyns was quite opposed to cutting the fruit, as the juice does have a way of running out nobody knows where.

Mary But there is a simple solution – pierce a hole in the orange and suck the juice –

(Miss Pole *stops* Mary.)

Miss Pole Miss Deborah did not like the term – (*Sotto.*) "suck". It does have an unpleasant association with that ceremony frequently undergone by little babies.

(*Enter* Miss Matty, *her orange in one hand and a skewer in the other, which she passes to* Miss Pole. Miss Pole *pierces a hole in the top of her orange and passes the skewer to* Mary. Mary *pierces her orange.* Miss Matty *takes the skewer and positions* Mary *in the middle of the garden.*)

Miss Matty You may be stationed here, my dear. Miss Pole, take your usual position.

(Miss Pole *hurries to stand on one side of* Mary. Miss Matty *stands on the other, forming a semi-circle.*)

Miss Matty Very well. We shall reconvene momentarily.

(Miss Matty *turns away.* Mary *looks to* Miss Pole *in confusion, who gestures for* Mary *to turn around.*)

Miss Pole (*to* Mary, *sotto*) A genius scheme instigated by Miss Deborah to allow each to indulge themselves in privacy without turning one's back on society. So to speak.

(MISS POLE, *then* MARY, *turn their backs. They suck their oranges, noisily.* THOMAS HOLBROOK *appears at the gate.* MARY *notices him.*)

MARY May I help you, sir?

(*The other women turn to look.* MISS MATTY *chokes on her orange juice.*)

THOMAS Miss Matilda Jenkyns! It cannot be!

(THOMAS *comes through the gate.*)

THOMAS God bless my soul, I should not have known you! How are you?

(MISS MATTY *is still coughing.*)

MARY She is well, sir.

THOMAS Miss Jenkyns, I never knew you had a daughter!

MARY I am Miss Matty's houseguest. And friend. Mary Smith.

THOMAS Delightful to meet you, my dear. I am Thomas Holbrook. My acquaintance with Miss Matilda dates many a year. And Miss Pole. Good day.

MISS MATTY (*having collected herself*) You are well, Mr Holbrook?

THOMAS You always were so very proper, Miss Jenkyns. Your sister Deborah must be quite proud.

MISS POLE Miss Deborah is not long gone from this world.

THOMAS (*to* MISS MATTY) Forgive me. I did not know. She must be greatly missed.

MISS MATTY She is.

THOMAS I fear I have imposed sadness. Allow me to make amends, invite you to my house. For tea. I hear ladies like tea.

MARY That is very kind, Mr Holbrook. We should be delighted. Where is your house?

THOMAS Miss Jenkyns knows.

(*Enter* MARTHA *with napkins.*)

MARTHA Here yer are, Miss Matilda, I've got napkins for yer sticky fingers –

(*She sees* THOMAS.)

MARTHA Mr Holbrook! Have yer got them cabbages?

THOMAS Some real beauties. I'll bring them through to the kitchen. Ladies, shall we say Tuesday week?

(*Exit* THOMAS.)

MISS MATTY Martha, go inside.

MARTHA Have I done wrong? He only supplies vegetables.

MISS POLE Cease your moaning and go inside, girl!

(*Exit* MARTHA.)

MISS MATTY I shall go within also.

(*Exit* MISS MATTY. MARY *goes to follow her.*)

MISS POLE She will prefer to be alone awhile. I have known her longer than you.

(*Exeunt, the other way.*)

Scene Three

Exterior. THOMAS HOLBROOK'S *garden on the outskirts of Cranford. Day.*

Enter THOMAS. *He sets up two chairs around a picnic rug, puts a picnic basket down and starts unpacking it. Enter* MISS MATTY, MISS POLE *and* MARY. MISS MATTY *is fiddling with her hat.*

MISS MATTY I am still unsure about this bonnet. Perhaps we should turn back.

MARY We are here! Mr Holbrook!

(THOMAS *looks up.*)

THOMAS Hullo!

MISS POLE (*sotto*) You would think he would at least have a drive to enable people to cross his garden without being jolted about so much!

MISS MATTY (*sotto*) I think it is very pretty.

THOMAS Come and sit down.

Miss Pole — I am afraid your mathematics is insufficient. There are four in our party.

Mary — A picnic! How delightful!

(Mary *gathers her skirts to sit down.*)

Miss Pole — (*in horror*) Miss Smith! Do not sit on the ground! You are sure to catch a severe chill and end up confined to your bed for the rest of the summer. Besides, ladies should not be seen scrabbling about on the floor.

(Mary *sits down.*)

Thomas — I'm afraid I am very set in the ways of the countryside. I don't know whether you like the new-fangled ways. We could retire to the parlour.

Miss Matty — I pay very little attention to fashion.

(Miss Pole *looks affronted, but sits as* Miss Matty *does, in a chair.* Thomas *sits on the rug and hands round a tray of food.*)

Miss Pole — How . . . quaint.

Miss Matty — Thank you. This is most kind.

Mary — Mr Holbrook, your garden is charming.

Thomas — It has been my dearest occupation for many years now. Should you like a tour?

Mary — (*simultaneously*) Oh, yes!

Miss Pole — (*simultaneously*) No, thank you!

MISS MATTY Miss Pole and I are quite comfortable here. But Mary – you must take a turn with Mr Holbrook.

(MARY *and* THOMAS *walk a little way off. He points things out to her.*)

MISS MATTY It is very pleasant dining with a bachelor. I only hope it is not improper, as so many pleasant things are.

MISS POLE (*looking at the picnic rug*) I am afraid he has got into very uncouth habits with living alone.

MISS MATTY Oh! Uncouth is too hard a word. I should call him eccentric. Very clever people always are.

MISS POLE I do not think sitting outside indicates particular intelligence! I can – (*She sniffs.*) – yes, without a doubt I can smell rain in the air! Come, we must go inside.

(*Exit* MISS POLE. MISS MATTY *stands. She sees* THOMAS *and* MARY *approach, freezes momentarily, and rushes inside. Exit* MISS MATTY.)

THOMAS I remember once, I arrived in the village still wearing my beekeeping outfit and – well, the ladies ran quite amok! Miss Pole was particularly vociferous I seem to recall.

MARY You and Miss Matty were good friends then?

(*The window of* THOMAS' *house slowly opens.* MISS MATTY *peers out.*)

THOMAS We were. I admired her above any other. But we have not spoken or even seen each other in thirty years.

MARY Why such a lengthy separation?

THOMAS I am afraid I could no longer stay in the village. But I have enjoyed my solitude ever since.

MARY What made you move?

THOMAS It is not for I to say, Miss Smith. I can tell you are a good friend to Miss Matty. Perhaps she will tell you in time. But allow me to request you inform her that my feelings . . . they have not changed one inch during this long interval to our acquaintance.

(MISS MATTY *gasps.* MARY *and* THOMAS *look round in alarm.*)

MISS MATTY There you are! I was just looking for you both, you've been gone quite some time!

MARY Is everything all right?

MISS MATTY Yes! Quite all right! Why would it not be? Now, are you coming inside? Miss Pole is growing quite restless for her tea.

THOMAS Actually, Miss Matty, I have been awaiting an opportunity to request a private audience with you.

MISS MATTY Oh! Oh, I am afraid that will not do, Mr Holbrook! We must return to the village before it grows dark.

MARY — But it is not yet three o'clock! Miss Pole and her tea –

MISS MATTY — Do you know, I think I was quite mistaken, I do not believe Miss Pole would like any more tea at all today. Mr Holbrook, thank you for your hospitality. Mary, hurry along!

(MISS MATTY *pulls the window shut. Exit* MARY, *not knowing what to say.* THOMAS *is crestfallen. He slowly walks over to the picnic area and packs up the rug and basket. Exit* THOMAS.)

Scene Four

Exterior. Cranford Village water pump. Day.

Enter MARTHA, *with a pail to fill with water. She goes to the pump. Enter* JEM *with a cup. He goes over to the pump.*

MARTHA — What do yer want?

(JEM *holds up his cup.*)

MARTHA — So yer dint just watch me come here from Miss Matty's?

JEM — I'm just here for water.

(MARTHA *steps back and allows* JEM *to fill his cup. He does so and drains it.*)

MARTHA — Thirsty work all that sittin round in the pub.

(MARTHA *goes back to filling the pail with water.*)

JEM — Yer could come and join me one time, if yer wanted.

(MARTHA *looks up at him in surprise. He turns away, mortified.* MARTHA *goes back to the pump, but struggles a little.* JEM *goes over to help her. She recoils a bit but he puts his hands over hers and pumps with her.*)

JEM — Yer just need ter put yer back into it.

(*They stop pumping and look at each other.* JEM *starts to lean in to kiss her. Enter* MISS MATTY *and* MARY, *returning home from visiting* THOMAS.)

MISS MATTY — (*in horror*) Martha!

(MARTHA *and* JEM *start away from each other, knocking the pail of water over.* MARTHA *hurries to pick it up.*)

MARTHA — Please, ma'am, he were just helpin' me –

MISS MATTY — Go home, Martha.

MARTHA — But Miss Matty –

MISS MATTY — Do not make me raise my voice, Martha. Go home. (*To* JEM.) And I do not wish to see you ever again, Mr Hearn. I forbid you to trouble my maid in future.

(MARTHA *bursts into tears and runs off. Exit* MARTHA. JEM *grabs the pail and runs after her. Exit* JEM.)

MISS MATTY — I wish that girl had more maidenly reserve.

MARY Perhaps it would not be so remiss if you were to relax your rules in this incidence. Martha seems like a steady young girl.

MISS MATTY She will not be so steady if she is three months confined! Deborah would have known what to do.

MARY Martha has not done anything reprehensible.

MISS MATTY No. No I am sure she has not. She is a good girl really. I just worry so much!

MARY We are women after all. That is our primary occupation.

(MISS MATTY *manages a small smile.*)

MARY What is wrong?

MISS MATTY This afternoon . . . I overheard your conversation with Mr Holbrook.

MARY Oh! Miss Matty, please do not be offended. I hope you do not think I spoke out of turn –

MISS MATTY Not at all. Mr Holbrook and I were once . . . romantically entangled. He-he asked me to marry him. I declined.

MARY You didn't love him?

MISS MATTY Quite the opposite!

MARY Then, why?

MISS MATTY He is a farmer. He would not have been a gentleman enough for my father. Or for Deborah.

MARY — But they were not to marry him!

MISS MATTY — I am a rector's daughter, Mary. I could not marry below my rank.

MARY — But Miss Matty – he told me – there is still time - his feelings have not altered!

MISS MATTY — But neither has my situation.

MARY — But Miss Deborah, she would not want you to be alone. Miss Matty, you do not have to leave the past as it is. There is always time to change.

(*Exeunt.*)

Scene Five

Exterior. The garden of CAPTAIN BROWN's *house. Day.*

Enter JESSIE *and* MISS BROWN. JESSIE *is supporting* MISS BROWN *as she coughs.*

JESSIE — Come, just a little further! The air will do you good! You have done so well, father will be so proud!

(MISS BROWN *coughs violently and* JESSIE *struggles to keep her standing. Enter* CAPTAIN BROWN *and* MAJOR GORDON, *laughing jovially and shaking hands.* CAPTAIN BROWN's *expression changes as he sees his daughter.*)

CAPT. BROWN — Mary, dear, how are you?

(MISS BROWN *descends into another coughing fit.*)

JESSIE	She is worse, father. I thought some fresh air would brighten her.
CAPT. BROWN	It was a kind enterprise. (*To* MISS BROWN.) Come, Mary, shall we play some cards inside?
	(*Exeunt* CAPTAIN BROWN *with* MISS BROWN.)
MAJ. GORDON	I am sorry your sister is so unwell.
JESSIE	I fear she is not long for this world.
MAJ. GORDON	It is that bad?
JESSIE	I don't like to think it, but what else can I do?
MAJ. GORDON	It cannot be easy for you.
JESSIE	It is a duty of care I willingly undertake.
MAJ. GORDON	Your mother would be proud.
	(JESSIE *is touched.*)
MAJ. GORDON	Miss Jessie, there is something I must ask you. It is a question I have long desired to ask, but I have held it within me for fear of seeming inattentive to your sister's plight. But your father assures me I may have cause to hope –
JESSIE	Please, do not say anything now that you may come to regret.
MAJ. GORDON	Regret? How could I ever regret this?
	(MAJOR GORDON *pulls out a small box from his pocket and bends onto one knee.*)

MAJ. GORDON Miss Brown, I have admired you for more years than I can say. It would give me the greatest pleasure if you would become my wife.

(JESSIE *is clearly thrilled but checks herself.*)

JESSIE My father –

MAJ. GORDON – has given his consent. I have seen the love with which you have tended to your father and sister. Now it is time you receive some affection.

(JESSIE'S *face falls and she turns away swiftly.*)

JESSIE I cannot give my consent, Major Gordon. Your proposal is most kind, but I am not in a position to marry.

MAJ. GORDON Do not think I wish to rip you from your family! Your father, your sister – they might live with us, or reside nearby –

JESSIE You are a military man. If I were to be a good wife to you, I would travel with you, accompany you everywhere. But I am in no position to do that.

MAJ. GORDON You would not need to! It would give me no greater pleasure than to return home to you –

JESSIE Then we would be forced into absence from each other. A marriage is about proximity.

MAJ. GORDON (*laughing*) It is about much more than that –

JESSIE I cannot marry you.

MAJ. GORDON — But why? Jessie, I know what is in your heart!

JESSIE — You do not.

MAJ. GORDON — You reject me only because of your sister! I know you love me!

JESSIE — I do not! I do not love you.

(MAJOR GORDON *takes a step back as though he has been hit.*)

MAJ. GORDON — Then it appears I am mistaken in my affection. I apologise for this misunderstanding, Miss Brown. I shall bid you good day.

(*Exit* MAJOR GORDON, *heartbroken. Exit* JESSIE, *the other way.*)

Scene Six

Exterior. The garden at MISS MATTY'S. *Day.*

Enter MISS MATTY *with a watering can. She attends to the flowers.*

MISS MATTY — Oh Deborah, I don't know what you would have made of Martha. Do you know, she put butter in the pastry and lard on the toast yesterday. Mary and I couldn't help laughing, there was nothing else for it. I think the poor girl must think me a dragon, the way she looks at me sometimes. You would have done the same to forbid her from seeing the carpenter. But you would have handled it much better than I. It took Mary three hours to stop her sobbing. I shall miss Mary when she returns home at the end of summer. She is indiscrete at times to be sure, but she is also wise. Much wiser than I. (*With sudden energy.*) Martha! Martha, could you come out here!

(*Enter* MARTHA.)

MISS MATTY Could you send a note to Mr Holbrook asking him to come by at his soonest convenience? There is something I would like to say to him.

MARTHA But Miss Matty – ain't yer heard? Mr Holbrook is gone from Cranford!

MISS MATTY Gone?

MARTHA Just this morning. Bound for Paris.

MISS MATTY He is going to France?

MARTHA I dunno, ma'am, he may well go there after he has been in Paris.

MISS MATTY He has gone alone?

MARTHA Major Gordon's regiment has been sent there, so Mr Holbrook took the opportunity ter travel with him. Captain Brown has gone as far as London with them too, on railway business. D'you know, ma'am, the village is brewin with rumours, a match was expected between Major Gordon and Jessie Brown –

MISS MATTY Ladies do not engage in idle gossip, Martha.

(MARTHA *bobs a curtsey and turns to go inside.*)

MISS MATTY Martha. You are young.

MARTHA Yes, ma'am. Two and twenty last third of October.

MISS MATTY And it seems you have met with a young man you like, who likes you. I did say you were not to have followers, but . . . I have no objection to Jem Hearn coming to see you once a week. God forbid that I should grieve any young hearts.

MARTHA Please, ma'am, if you ask about him tomorrow morning, everyone will give him a character for steadiness; and he'll be glad enough to come tomorrow night, I'll be bound!

(MARTHA *starts to rush off, but looks back.*)

MARTHA Thank you, Miss Matty, ma'am.

(*Exit* MARTHA.)

MISS MATTY (*to Deborah*) Thomas always had a wish to go to Paris. But I must say, I do not believe frogs will agree with him.

(*Enter* JESSIE, *sobbing.*)

JESSIE Miss Matty!

MISS MATTY Jessie, dear! What is it?

JESSIE Miss Matty, I am so sorry – I didn't know who else to turn to – my father is gone and I –

MISS MATTY Speak calmly, my dear and tell me what has happened.

JESSIE It is my sister! It is Mary! She – she is dead!

(JESSIE *descends into sobs in* MISS MATTY'S *arms.* MISS MATTY *holds her, then leads her gently away. Exeunt* MISS MATTY *and* JESSIE.)

ACT THREE

Scene One

Exterior. The garden of MISS POLE'S *house. Day.*

Enter MISS POLE. *She is carrying sheets of newspaper, which she places wherever the sun shines. Enter* MARY.

MISS POLE Thank goodness you have come! Quick – help me!

(MISS POLE *shoves newspaper at* MARY.)

MISS POLE Take that area. Be diligent!

MARY But what am I to do?

MISS POLE I would have thought that would be clear. I have just had new paving slabs laid.

MARY They are most becoming.

MISS POLE But they shall not remain so if these insensitive sunbeams have their way. They will fade the colour straight to white, Miss Smith! We must arrange the papers to protect the stones from the blaze.

(MARY *begins to walk to her designated area.*)

MISS POLE Miss Smith, you need not tarnish the stones unnecessarily. The grass is quite clean enough to be trod upon.

(MARY *walks around the paving stones. Both women chase sunbeams with newspaper.*)

Miss Pole: Miss Matty is still with the girl?

Mary: She was inconsolable when I left.

Miss Pole: Miss Matty?

Mary: Jessie.

Miss Pole: I cannot bear to hear a young girl cry. One day she will be old and she will look back and regret these hours spent wailing over nothing.

Mary: She has just lost her sister.

Miss Pole: And her senses too! Imagine – a woman walking behind the funeral party without a male chauffeur! And to drag Miss Matty down with her.

(*Enter* Miss Matty, *unseen.*)

Mary: It was no disgrace. Miss Matty did it gladly. She did not wish Jessie to bear the trial alone.

Miss Matty: It would not have been fit for her to go alone. It would have been against propriety and humanity if I had allowed it.

(Miss Matty *starts walking across the paving stones.*)

Miss Pole: Miss Matty! Retreat and pause! Be not so rash, I beg you!

(Miss Pole *gestures to* Mary *for her papers.* Mary *passes them.* Miss Pole *makes a path across the stones with newspaper.*)

MISS POLE Now you may progress.

(MISS MATTY *walks across the newspaper stepping stones.*)

MARY How is she?

MISS MATTY Tired. She will sleep soundly despite her distress.

(*From offstage, the sound of a hunting horn.*)

MISS POLE Mrs Jamieson! She has not called since the debacle at the village meeting!

(MISS POLE *quickly picks up the newspaper.*)

MISS MATTY I should think Mrs Jamieson's boots are just as dirty as ours.

MARY And Mr Mulliner's certainly are.

MISS POLE That maybe so, but this is one economy I care not for Mrs Jamieson to witness. Imagine what she might think? Or worse, what she might say!

(*Enter* MR MULLINER, *who blows the hunting horn again.*)

MR MULLINER The Honourable Mrs Jamieson.

(*Enter* MRS JAMIESON, *holding Carlo in her arms, who has a cardboard cone around his neck.*)

MARY Oh Carlo!

MRS JAMIESON He is still in recovery from that vicious attack by that nasty, sickly girl.

(*Enter* JESSIE. *She has clearly been crying.* MRS JAMIESON *does not see her.*)

MRS JAMIESON I knew she had a snide look in her eye the moment I saw her. She took one look at my Carlo and singled him out as the target of her cruel ministrations.

MARY I really don't think –

MRS JAMIESON Miss Smith, I have met people who do not like dogs before. They are uniformly blind to the unnaturalness of their dislike of our canine companions. They will stop at nothing to make their discontent known and to seek revenge on any poor, innocent creature they set eyes upon! I can only hope that her father saw it fit to exact punishment for such blatant disregard for man's faithfullest friend. What has become of the girl?

JESSIE She is dead.

(MRS JAMIESON *looks around and sees* JESSIE.)

JESSIE My sister died, Mrs Jamieson. But at least now I can be sure she did not die in vain. Dog lovers everywhere may seek consolation in her demise.

MISS MATTY (*to* JESSIE) Have you had word from your father?

JESSIE He is to return home as soon as possible. He has cut his work short.

MARY What about Major Gordon?

JESSIE He is still in Paris, I believe.

MRS JAMIESON How ghastly! Who would want to go to that wicked place? They are always having revolutions. I hope he does not return with ideas above his station. (*To* JESSIE.) It is rather a shame you refused his offer of marriage.

JESSIE I did not realise my love life was the subject of village gossip, Mrs Jamieson.

MRS JAMIESON It is not. The lack of it, however, is.

JESSIE Then why is it such a shame I refused him? Surely this simply fuelled your appetite for the macabre?

MRS JAMIESON You refused him on account of your sister's ill health. Now that obstacle has been removed.

JESSIE I am sure that my sister shall be happy to no longer burden my romantic hopes from beyond the grave.

(JESSIE *turns away, angry and offended.*)

MRS JAMIESON Mulliner, do you have the invitations?

MISS POLE Invitations?

MRS JAMIESON To a garden party, next week.

(MR MULLINER *hands round invitations.*)

MISS MATTY Is it not Mrs Forrester's turn to host?

MRS JAMIESON Yes, but she does insist on serving sandwiches with the crusts left on. They give poor Carlo such indigestion, don't they, poppit? She seemed offended when I told her. I cannot think why.

(MRS JAMIESON *turns to go.*)

MISS POLE Good day, Mrs Jamieson!

(*Exeunt* MRS JAMIESON *and* MR MULLINER.)

JESSIE I don't understand how my refusal of Major Gordon came to be public knowledge. I acted with the utmost discretion.

(JESSIE *begins pacing.* MISS POLE *dashes around her, placing newspaper sheets on the floor, trying to anticipate where* JESSIE *will step.*)

MISS MATTY I am afraid things have a way of happening like that in Cranford.

JESSIE In Cranford! Why must everything have it's own special way in Cranford?

MISS POLE Oh, what is the use?

(MISS POLE *gives up trying to protect her paving stones.*)

MISS MATTY (*to* MISS POLE) Come inside and leave the sun to do its irrepressible work.

MISS POLE But the paving stones will soon be quite as white as yours! No offence, my dear.

(MISS POLE *allows herself to be pulled away. Exeunt* MISS POLE *and* MISS MATTY.)

JESSIE — I do not know what I am to do without her.

MARY — I have never had a sister, so I can only imagine your loss. But from my slender experience of grief, it will ease and lessen with every day that passes.

(JESSIE *turns, crying.* MARY *embraces her.*)

MARY — I know Cranford seems strange in its ways and customs, but it is a place full of love and kindness.

JESSIE — Even Mrs Jamieson?

MARY — Technically she does live just beyond the bounds of the village.

(*They share a smile.*)

CAPT. BROWN — (*offstage*) Jessie! Jessie!

JESSIE — It can't be!

(*Enter* CAPTAIN BROWN *with a suitcase.*)

CAPT. BROWN — Jessie!

JESSIE — Father!

(*She runs to him and they embrace.*)

JESSIE — I feared it might be days yet before you could return.

CAPT. BROWN — Did she suffer much?

JESSIE — No, father. She was so very brave. And when she had gone, it looked as though she simply slept. She is more peaceful now than she has been for many years.

CAPT. BROWN I am so sorry you had to bear this burden alone, child.

JESSIE I have not been alone.

(JESSIE *turns to look at* MARY. CAPTAIN BROWN *notices her.*)

CAPT. BROWN Miss Smith, you will hold high regard in my eyes forever for the friendship you have offered my Jessie.

(*Enter* MISS MATTY.)

MISS MATTY Captain Brown!

CAPT. BROWN Miss Matilda. Allow me to thank you for your attentions to my daughter during my absence. I have a gift – to express my thanks.

(CAPTAIN BROWN *opens his case.*)

MISS MATTY That is most unnecessary.

(CAPTAIN BROWN *presents* MISS MATTY *with a carved wooden coal shovel.*)

CAPT. BROWN I recall you said your sister always desired one.

MISS MATTY This is most finely crafted.

CAPT. BROWN It was delicate work.

MISS MATTY You carved it yourself?

(CAPTAIN BROWN *inclines his head.*)

MISS MATTY Thank you, captain. You must join Mary and I for tea. You will want to see the shovel in its rightful place, will you not?

(*Exit* MISS MATTY. CAPTAIN BROWN *smiles and picks up his case, puts his arm around* JESSIE. *He gestures for* MARY *to precede them. Exeunt.*)

Scene Two

Exterior. The garden at MRS JAMIESON'S. *Day.*

Enter MR MULLINER, *who arranges the chairs and puts plates of food on the table. He checks the coast is clear before taking a bite out of a pork pie. He relishes it.*

MISS POLE (*offstage*) Lift your skirts, Mary, you are dragging them in the mud!

(*Hearing the ladies approaching,* MR MULLINER *looks for somewhere to conceal the half-eaten pie. Enter* MISS POLE, MISS MATTY, MARY *and* JESSIE. MISS MATTY *is wearing a widow's cap.* MR MULLINER *turns his back and stuffs the pie down his trousers. He looks around.*)

MISS POLE Where is Mrs Jamieson?

MR MULLINER Her ladyship is preparing herself.

(*He gives a curt bow. Exit* MR MULLINER.)

MISS POLE Quickly, Miss Matty, there is time to change your cap!

MISS MATTY I am quite comfortable, thank you.

MISS POLE But it is a widow's cap! Mary, don't you think it looks like a widow's cap? Why would you wear such a thing? Mary will swap with you, won't you dear?

MISS MATTY There is no need.

(*Enter* MR MULLINER *with* MRS FORRESTER. MRS FORRESTER *cradles her cat in her arms.*)

MR MULLINER Mrs Forrester. Do sit down.

(*Exit* MR MULLINER.)

MRS FORRESTER What did he say? He mumbles terribly.

MISS POLE Come and sit down!

MRS FORRESTER Hmmm, what was that?

MISS POLE (*louder*) Sit down!

MRS FORRESTER Hmmm?

MISS POLE (*louder still*) Sit down!

MRS FORRESTER No need to shout, dear!

MARY (*loudly, looking at the cat*) Who is this?

MRS FORRESTER You could not have forgotten me, I am sure!

MARY I meant your cat.

MRS FORRESTER My hat? It does not have a name. Oh! You mean Pussy-Wilkins!

JESSIE Pussy . . . Wilkins?

MISS MATTY Named after her husband.

MISS POLE And the less said about him the better. (*Loudly.*) That is a lovely name, Mrs Forrester.

MARY And what a good boy he is.

(MARY *reaches out to stroke the cat, who hisses and spits.*)

MRS FORRESTER Hear how he croons at you, dear! He likes you. I am afraid he has grown quite nervous in his old age. I simply cannot leave him alone in the house these days. After I came home to find all my stockings ripped to shreds and Rodgers the owl torn to pieces on the parlour rug, I knew I could not leave poor pussy alone again.

JESSIE (*in alarm*) Rodgers the owl?

MISS POLE Stuffed.

MRS FORRESTER He has never been quite the same since. (*To* JESSIE.) My dear, I don't think we have been introduced.

MISS POLE This is Miss Jessie Brown.

MRS FORRESTER Pleased to meet you. I see you have blonde hair. I find girls who have blonde hair are often well travelled. Have you travelled much, Miss Crown?

JESSIE Yes, I have an uncle – my mother's brother – who is a shopkeeper in Edinburgh. We visited him a few times when I was younger.

MISS POLE (*sotto, to* MARY) I do wish Miss Brown would have a little more self-control. What will Mrs Forrester do now she has heard she is in company with a shopkeeper's niece?

MARY I don't think there is much danger of Mrs Forrester having heard that.

MRS FORRESTER It is a shame you have never visited Edinburgh. But if you do go, I should not worry about visiting shopkeepers very much. They are quite objectionable on the whole.

(*Enter* MR MULLINER *and* MRS JAMIESON, *holding Carlo in her arms. She is wearing a dress with a large lace collar.*)

MR MULLINER The Honourable Mrs Jamieson.

MRS JAMIESON I hope you have saved your banter for my arrival, ladies.

(MRS JAMIESON *sits next to* MRS FORRESTER. *As soon as Carlo and Pussy-Wilkins see each other, they start yelping and hissing at each other.*)

MRS JAMIESON Carlo! Come to mama, my poppit! Mrs Forrester, what occasion could you possibly have had to bring that . . . that beast . . . here?

MRS FORRESTER Pussy-Wilkins is so pleased to see little Carlo again!

MRS JAMIESON I am sure you will excuse me if I give my poor Carlo his tea first.

(MRS JAMIESON *pours some tea and cream into a saucer.*)

MRS JAMIESON He is such an intelligent and sensible little fellow. He knows cream quite well, and always refuses tea with milk in it.

(MRS JAMIESON *puts the saucer down and allows Carlo to drink.*)

MRS FORRESTER Is there cream enough left for my Pussy-Wilkins?

MRS JAMIESON No. Pass the milk, dear.

(MRS JAMIESON *pours tea and passes the milk jug to* MARY. *She pours herself some, then hands it round.*)

MARY I am glad to see Carlo no longer has to wear his cone.

(MRS JAMIESON *shushes her.*)

MRS JAMIESON He grows most distressed when that article of attire is mentioned. (*To* MISS MATTY.) I saw that serving girl of yours yesterday, Miss Matty. She was being most promiscuous on the village green. Holding hands! With a man! How proud you must be that she is sowing her seeds around the village.

MRS FORRESTER You possess a maid who gardens, Miss Matty? A fortunate acquisition indeed! Does she keep it well pruned?

MISS POLE I am afraid she is rather distracted by attending to the bushy wildernesses of Cranford's bachelors.

Miss Matty — Martha has only one follower, and she seems quite united with him. Although . . .

Miss Pole — Yes?

Miss Matty — There was an incident last night which made me rather uncomfortable. I retired early, but found myself quite unable to sleep, so I stepped down to the kitchen to ask Martha to warm some milk. When I found it deserted, I assumed she had finished her jobs and retired also. But just as I was turning to go, I heard a strange noise.

Mrs Jamieson — Where?

Miss Matty — In the street, just outside the door. It sounded like . . . well, it sounded like . . .

Mary — Talking?

Miss Matty — No. Kissing!

Miss Pole — (*in horror*) Kissing!

(*As the women express their horror, Carlo starts to sniff the air.*)

Mrs Forrester — Who has gone missing?

Miss Pole — (*loudly*) Kissing! In the street!

Mrs Forrester — How disgusting! Miss Pole, I am quite shocked you would use such a word. But I must say, it explains that terrible stench that lingers in the village. These young men should learn to use the latrine!

Mary — (*louder still*) No, Mrs Forrester, kissing!

MRS FORRESTER (*in shock*) Oh. I did not think it could get worse.

MRS JAMIESON (*to* MISS MATTY) This is just the start of your problems. Mark my words.

(*Carlo locates the source of the smell as* MR MULLINER'S *crotch – the pork pie. Carlo launches himself at* MR MULLINER'S *crotch, yapping excitedly.* MRS JAMIESON *fights to control Carlo as he sniffs around* MR MULLINER'S *crotch.*)

MRS JAMIESON Carlo! Carlo, control yourself! I don't know what has come over him! He's usually such a good boy!

(MR MULLINER *backs off. The half eaten pie rolls out from his trousers.*)

MR MULLINER Ma'am, I can explain. This is not how it appears . . .

(MRS JAMIESON *bursts out laughing.*)

MRS JAMIESON Carlo, what a clever boy you are! He still has that streak of wildness about him, always so ready to forage out a snack! Here, Mulliner, take him inside and let him enjoy his reward.

(MR MULLINER *picks up the pie and takes Carlo from* MRS JAMIESON. *Exit* MR MULLINER *with Carlo.*)

MRS JAMIESON He is such a lively little thing! I would never be without him. You have never had a pet, have you, Matilda?

Miss Matty My sister did not care for animal hair in the house. She believed that beasts of the field belong in the field.

Mrs Jamieson Carlo has never had to see a field! I don't suppose the same can be said of your Pussy-Wilkins, Mrs Forrester. I suppose he is always going from paddock to meadow looking for the next chase.

Mrs Forrester Pussy-Wilkins has no taste for lace. I, however, quite adore it. That collar you are wearing is most exquisite.

Mrs Jamieson It is the sole relic of better days. Such lace cannot be got now for either love or money. It was made by nuns. Abroad. I treasure my lace very much. I daren't even trust the washing of it to my maid.

Miss Pole You don't . . . wash it yourself?

Mrs Jamieson I do, and I am not too proud to admit it. I have a recipe for washing it in milk, which gives it a very good creamy colour. It is entirely of my own creation. I suppose it would not be too much of an inconvenience for me to show you.

Miss Pole Mrs Forrester? (*Louder.*) Mrs Forrester?

Mrs Forrester Hmmm?

Miss Pole Should you like to see Mrs Jamieson's lace be washed?

Mrs Forrester No I should not! Who on earth would try to squash poor Mrs Jamieson's face?

(MISS POLE *pulls a confused* MRS FORRESTER *up*.)

MISS POLE — Miss Matty? Perhaps seeing this method may tempt you to give your old lace cap another chance?

MISS MATTY — I shall remain here with the girls and finish my tea.

(*Exeunt* MRS JAMIESON, MISS POLE *and* MRS FORRESTER.)

MARY — (*to* MISS MATTY) You do not have to change your cap for anyone.

MISS MATTY — No. I do not. Miss Brown, I wonder if you recall from your time in London – are turbans in fashion?

JESSIE — Yes, I believe they were.

MISS MATTY — I should so like a great Saracen's turban. Perhaps I shall try to get one before the Midsummer party.

JESSIE — A party?

MISS MATTY — A very jolly occasion when we celebrate the coming of summer after so many months of quiet solemnity in the village.

(*From offstage, there is the sudden sound of a violent kerfuffle – Pussy-Wilkins hissing and spitting, Carlo barking and* MRS JAMIESON, MRS FORRESTER *and* MISS POLE *screeching in horror*.)

MISS MATTY — Good heavens!

MARY — You don't think someone really has tried to squash Mrs Jamieson's face?

(*Enter* MISS POLE, *breathless. The sounds offstage continue.*)

MISS POLE — It is Pussy-Wilkins! He has – swallowed the lace!

JESSIE — Is he all right?

MISS POLE — He is choking, as befits such a heinous offence.

JESSIE — Oh!

MISS POLE — Never mind about him – the lace, Miss Brown, the lace!

MISS MATTY — Miss Pole, calm yourself. Precisely what happened?

MISS POLE — We followed Mrs Jamieson's instructions – filled a shallow bowl with milk and laid the lace out flat, then stepped back to allow the colour restoration to begin. It was just as Mrs Jamieson and I were discussing our outfits for the Midsummer party that Mrs Forrester gave a very startled cry. We did not think much of it, suspecting she had misheard something as usual, but when we turned – Pussy-Wilkins had leapt from her arms and emptied the bowl of milk and lace and all! Miss Matty, I beg you accompany me for some tartar emetic. To advance the natural proceedings. (*To* MARY *and* JESSIE.) Go directly to the store and request Mr Johnson lend us one of his top-boots for an hour. But – care he suspect not what its use shall be.

JESSIE Its use?

MARY I think it is to be a receiving vessel.

JESSIE (*in horror*) Oh!

(*Exeunt* MARY *and* JESSIE *in one direction,* MISS MATTY *and* MISS POLE *in the other.*)

Scene Three

Exterior. Cranford Village Green. Day.

Enter MARTHA *and* JEM*, arm in arm.*

MARTHA So when yer gonna ask me ter make an honest man of yer then?

JEM What?

MARTHA My mistress has been asking, yer know.

JEM She has?

MARTHA She's quite determined, yer know, not ter have an unmarried gal with a follower in her kitchen for long!

JEM Oh . . . well, I, er –

MARTHA I'm teasin' yer, yer big oaf! Ain't never seen yer look so scared. Though I ain't sure I should take that as a compliment! Maybe I should start ter doubt yer affection for me!

JEM I'll show yer doubt.

(Jem *grabs* Martha *and kisses her. Enter* Miss Matty *and* Miss Pole. Miss Matty *sees* Martha *and* Jem *and stops.*)

Miss Pole — Hurry, Miss Matty! Goodness knows what state Mrs Jamieson's lace is in by now!

Miss Matty — Martha!

(Martha *and* Jem *break apart.*)

Martha — Miss Matty, ma'am!

(*She rushes over, trying to distract attention from* Jem.)

Martha — Eh! Ter think of yer goin out in such a thin shawl! At yer age, ma'am, yer should be careful.

Miss Matty — My age! Why, how old do you think I am?

Martha — Well, ma'am, I should say yer were not short of sixty. But folks' looks is often against them and I'm sure I meant no harm.

Miss Matty — Martha, I'm not yet fifty-two.

Jem — Yer don't look a day over fifty, ma'am.

Miss Matty — Mr Hearn, you need not use flattery to recommend yourself to me, I assure you.

(*Enter* Jessie *and* Mary *with a boot.*)

Mary — We have it!

Jessie — And you will never guess what we saw in the store! A magic show is coming to town!

MARY Tomorrow night!

JESSIE With a real conjuror!

MISS POLE If you want to see magic you need only follow me back to Mrs Jamieson and Pussy-Wilkins, my girl. Come along!

(*Exeunt* MISS POLE, MISS MATTY, MARY *and* JESSIE. JEM *goes to grab* MARTHA *again*.)

MARTHA Worra yer doin? We'll hafta get tickets now before they sell out!

(MARTHA *turns, then looks back, grabs* JEM *and kisses him. She releases him and leaves, followed by a stunned* JEM. *Exeunt*.)

Scene Four

Exterior. Cranford Village water pump. Day.

Enter MRS JAMIESON, MISS POLE, MISS MATTY, MARY *and* JESSIE. *Between them, they hold the boot and several buckets. They rush over to the pump and pump water into the boot.*

MRS JAMIESON Quickly, quickly, I beg you!

(JESSIE *goes to turn the boot upside down*.)

MRS JAMIESON Not in the middle of the street! Here – over the wall.

(*The women rush to the wall and turn the boot upside down. They look – and are all disturbed by what they see*.)

MRS JAMIESON (*faintly*) More water. Quickly!

(*The women rush back to the pump and form a line to pass the buckets to* MRS JAMIESON *as they are filled, who pours water over the lace behind the wall.*)

MRS JAMIESON If we keep soaking it, some of the damage may be immediately undone.

MISS POLE Then lay it upon a lavender bush in the sun.

JESSIE Why a lavender bush?

MISS POLE To counteract the . . . aroma.

MISS MATTY Then we will put it in milk again.

MARY Far away from the reach of Pussy-Wilkins!

MISS POLE No one will ever guess it has been in pussy's insides.

(MRS JAMIESON *holds up a hand to stop the buckets. She leans down, then holds up a dirty brown piece of lace.*)

MRS JAMIESON It will never be the same again!

(MRS JAMIESON *flings the lace down and rushes off. Exit* MRS JAMIESON.)

MISS POLE Some boiling water will have quite miraculous results, I assure you!

(MISS POLE *gingerly deposits the lace in a bucket.*)

MISS POLE We shall have Mrs Forrester to thank if Mrs Jamieson never speaks to us again!

(*Exeunt.*)

Scene Five

Exterior. Cranford Village Green. Day.

Enter SIGNOR BRUNONI. *He wears a brightly coloured turkish outfit and a turban. He speaks with a strong accent.*

SIGNOR BRUN. Ladies and gentlemen, boys and girls! Welcome! Welcome to this – the most mysterious, most miraculous, most magnificent magic show the world has never seen!

(*Enter* MRS JAMIESON, MISS MATTY, MARY, MISS POLE, JESSIE, CAPTAIN BROWN, MARTHA *and* JEM. MRS JAMIESON *is holding Carlo. They gather around to watch.*)

MISS POLE He does not look at all like a conjuror ought to look.

MISS MATTY (*to* MARY) You see, my dear, turbans are worn.

SIGNOR BRUN. I, your humble servant, am here to entertain and delight you with spectacles and tricks unequal to any you have seen before!

(SIGNOR BRUNONI *pulls a bunch of flowers out of his sleeve with a flourish and presents them to* MARY.)

MISS POLE (*to* MARY) He will be trying to saw you in half next.

SIGNOR BRUN. (*to* MISS POLE) Madam, I would attempt no such knavery. I am a professional of the lowest order!

MRS JAMIESON The lowest? That is correct!

Signor Brun. Ah, how do you say – the highest order? Forgive me, my English, it not so good. But you want a traditional English trick?

(Signor Brunoni *takes off his turban with a flourish and holds it out, gesturing for* Jessie *to reach inside. She pulls out a miniature white rabbit.*)

Jessie (*in delight*) Father, may I keep it?

Capt. Brown Jessie, dear, my allergies!

Miss Matty (*to* Miss Pole) That was impressive, you must admit.

(Captain Brown *sneezes as* Jessie *tries to show him the rabbit.*)

Signor Brun. Sir! Allow me to assist.

(Signor Brunoni *pulls a row of handkerchiefs from his sleeve, which he hands to* Captain Brown, *much to the ladies' delight. He finally pulls out another bunch of flowers which he presents to* Martha.)

Jem Worra yer mean by givin' flowers to my gal? She'll get all the flowers she needs from me!

(Jem *snatches the flowers and throws them at* Signor Brunoni.)

Martha (*in horror*) Jem!

Jem Yer told me I had to stick up for yer honour!

Martha Not by embarrassin' me in front o' the whole village!

(MARTHA *storms off.*)

JEM — Martha! I had to pay two weeks' wages for them there seats!

(JEM *runs after her. Exeunt* MARTHA *and* JEM.)

SIGNOR BRUN. — The course of true love, it always did run smooth. (*To* MRS JAMIESON, *flirtaciously.*) But perhaps we can straighten its path?

(*He offers the flowers to her.* MRS JAMIESON *giggles girlishly.*)

MRS JAMIESON — No, I couldn't possibly.

SIGNOR BRUN. — (*withdrawing the flowers*) Very well, I respect a lady's wishes –

(MRS JAMIESON *quickly snatches the flowers.*)

MRS JAMIESON — I suppose I could take them off your hands.

SIGNOR BRUN. — But who is this fine creature?

MRS JAMIESON — This is my bella Carlo.

SIGNOR BRUN. — Ah! Young Carlo! He is just the kind of brave young fellow I require to assist me in my next trick!

MRS JAMIESON — Oh, no, Carlo does not like magic at all.

SIGNOR BRUN. — I am sure we could convince him. Perhaps he might like some of these very fine Turkish chocolates?

(SIGNOR BRUNONI *pulls out chocolates and offers one to an eager Carlo.*)

MRS JAMIESON And perhaps, his mistress may like one also?

(*He offers a chocolate to* MRS JAMIESON *who takes it with a giggle.*)

MRS JAMIESON It seems you have persuaded us, Signor.

SIGNOR BRUN. Excellent!

(SIGNOR BRUNONI *takes Carlo from* MRS JAMIESON. *He retrieves a large box.*)

SIGNOR BRUN. Now, I shall amaze and enthral you with my most terrible trick yet!

MISS MATTY (*sotto*) It is most distracting when he confuses his words. Surely he means "terrific"?

MISS POLE We do not know if he meant that or not yet.

SIGNOR BRUN. A disappearing act!

MRS JAMIESON Oh, no! Carlo has changed his mind!

SIGNOR BRUN. It is perfectly safe. You have my word.

(*He bows low over* MRS JAMIESON'S *hand and kisses it. She giggles.* SIGNOR BRUNONI *places Carlo on the floor and puts the box over him.*)

SIGNOR BRUN. Ladies and gentlemen, this is a very old trick from my native country and requires my utmost concentration as I utter these magical words – aber romata cromio regina aberacadabra hola quita requiosa!

(SIGNOR BRUNONI *gives an exaggerated flourish of his arms over the box.*)

SIGNOR BRUN. And now you will see how Carlo the dog has disappeared behind your very eyes!

(SIGNOR BRUNONI *lifts the box up triumphantly – Carlo is gone. His audience burst into applause.*)

SIGNOR BRUN. I thank you, I thank you!

MRS JAMIESON Now bring him back.

(SIGNOR BRUNONI *replaces the box and performs another elaborate hand flourish.*)

SIGNOR BRUN. Rabbi ata monita contrabracadabra Juanita magistration requiatum!

(SIGNOR BRUNONI *lifts the box. The space beneath is empty.*)

MRS JAMIESON Where is he?

SIGNOR BRUN. (*covering his unease*) It is all part of the magic! Misdirection, ladies! I had you convinced, didn't I, that poor Carlo was lost to the world! But it is not so!

(SIGNOR BRUNONI *puts the box back down.*)

SIGNOR BRUN. Omni ata ravi contra regorgio.

(SIGNOR BRUNONI *lifts the box again. The space beneath is empty.*)

MRS JAMIESON (*in distress*) Where is he? Carlo? Carlo, come to mama!

CAPT. BROWN Sir, I think you should desist this charade. Can you not see this poor woman is distressed?

(SIGNOR BRUNONI *puts the box down again and performs an even more elaborate and slightly frenzied flourish.*)

SIGNOR BRUN. Ta-dah!

(SIGNOR BRUNONI *lifts the box with a flourish. Carlo lies beneath on his back, all four legs stuck up in the air.* MRS JAMIESON *gasps, and then throws herself upon the dog.*)

MRS JAMIESON Carlo! Carlo! He is . . . dead!

SIGNOR BRUN. No! He is simply sleeping! See, wake up, doggy!

(SIGNOR BRUNONI *nudges Carlo with a foot. Carlo's body rolls over.* CAPTAIN BROWN *pushes through the crowd and crouches over the dog. He checks to see if it is breathing.*)

CAPT. BROWN Mrs Jamieson. I am so sorry for your loss.

MRS JAMIESON No! No, it is too much! (*To* SIGNOR BRUNONI.) You murdering blackguard!

(MRS JAMIESON *howls and falls upon* CAPTAIN BROWN, *cradling the dead Carlo in her arms.*)

MISS MATTY Mary, quickly, go to the medicine cabinet at home and fetch a restorative. She is quite beside herself. The smelling salts!

(*Exit* MARY.)

MISS POLE (*to* SIGNOR BRUNONI) Precisely what do you intend to do about this?

SIGNOR BRUN. What can I say? I am simply a vehicle of the Lord our God. If he has taken our poor brother Carlo to the doggy heaven on high, then who are we to question his ways?

(SIGNOR BRUNONI *backs away. As the women advance on him, he turns and runs. Exit* SIGNOR BRUNONI.)

MRS JAMIESON It is too much!

(MRS JAMIESON *swoons.* CAPTAIN BROWN *is there to support her.*)

MISS POLE (*sotto*) Mrs Jamieson seems to have warmed very quickly to Captain Brown.

(*Enter* MARY *with smelling salts.*)

MISS POLE Quickly, I shall administer the remedy.

(MISS POLE *holds the salts under* MRS JAMIESON'S *nose. She is revived.*)

MRS JAMIESON Where am I? Oh, Captain!

CAPT. BROWN Madam, I must release you into the care of your friends so I might pursue that rogue. Excuse me.

(*Exit* CAPTAIN BROWN.)

MRS JAMIESON Perhaps it is not such a bad thing to have a gentleman in Cranford.

MISS POLE Mrs Jamieson, you are quite unwell and do not know what you are saying. We shall escort you home.

(*Exeunt.*)

ACT FOUR

Scene One

Exterior. Cranford Village Green. Day.

Enter Mrs Jamieson, *holding a small coffin. A procession of* Miss Matty, Miss Pole, Mary, Jessie *and* Captain Brown *follows behind.* Mrs Jamieson *tearfully puts the coffin down and they form a semi-circle around.*

Mrs Jamieson — Captain Brown, I wondered if you might say a few words. You tried so hard to avenge his death.

Capt. Brown — Dear Carlo, friend of all animals –

Mary — (*sotto*) Except for Mrs Forrester's cat.

Capt. Brown — He lived a long and full life, and no creature could be happier to have spent his days basking in the warm glow of Mrs Jamieson's love and affection.

(Mrs Jamieson *lets out a sob.*)

Capt. Brown — But now, his barking days are over, and our old friend shall be remembered fondly by all who knew him. Rest in peace, dear Carlo, until that time when you may meet your mistress once more. Amen.

Mrs Jamieson — That was beautiful. Now we must remain in silent contemplation.

Mary — But the milliner and dressmaker are in town!

MRS JAMIESON How can you think of such things at a time like this?

MISS MATTY The distraction may cheer you.

MRS JAMIESON I shall never be cheerful again. And I shall never been seen in anything but black again. If you are all intent on such disrespect, you may escort me home, Captain Brown.

(MRS JAMIESON *takes* CAPTAIN BROWN *by the arm. Exeunt* MRS JAMIESON *and* CAPTAIN BROWN. *Enter a* MILLINER, *who starts setting up her stall. The women wander over. Enter a* GENTLEMAN, *who peruses the* MILLINER'S *selection.*)

MISS MATTY Miss Pole, are you well? You have been quite silent.

MARY Are you not excited at the prospect of a new dress pattern?

MISS POLE What does it signify how we dress here at Cranford where everybody knows us?

JESSIE I am sure we shall find something to suit you.

MISS POLE I am afraid you shall not. I am quite inconsolable today.

(*They have arrived at the* MILLINER'S *stall. A bonnet catches* MISS POLE'S *eye.*)

MISS POLE I suppose this is tolerably pretty.

MARY It would go very well with your blue shawl.

MISS POLE Oh, no, if I were to buy this, I would have to purchase an entirely new outfit. Which would be very tiresome.

(MISS POLE *turns away, then abruptly reaches for the hat at the same time as the* GENTLEMAN. *He steps back.*)

GENTLEMAN I shall make another selection.

MISS POLE I have no interest in the hat, I assure you.

(*The* GENTLEMAN *smiles pleasantly and takes the hat.*)

MISS POLE Well, there is nothing I will buy now.

MARY He offered you the hat.

MISS POLE What interest do I have in a hat that appealed to a man's taste?

MISS MATTY Mary, look! They have a turban!

(MISS MATTY *takes up the turban and quickly unties her bonnet.*)

MISS POLE Are you sure you wish to try it, Matty dear? It is awfully masculine.

(MISS MATTY *gives* MARY *her bonnet and places the turban on her head. It looks ridiculous.*)

MISS MATTY Does it look well?

MARY (*diplomatically*) You carry it admirably.

(MISS POLE *is unable to stifle her laughter.*)

MARY — Miss Pole!

MISS POLE — Forgive me. But it is not becoming for a lady. Do take it off, Matty dear.

MARY — If you like it, we shall buy it, Miss Matty.

MISS MATTY — Perhaps I should continue to wear caps, like all the other ladies in Cranford.

(MISS MATTY *removes the turban and puts her bonnet back on. The* GENTLEMAN *gives the* MILLINER *payment for his hat.*)

MILLINER — Town and County bank? We received a warning against notes issued by this bank just this morning. I'm afraid I must ask for payment in cash.

(*The* GENTLEMAN *checks his money bag and takes his bank note back. He gives the hat to the* MILLINER, *thanks her and steps away, looking concerned.*)

JESSIE — Your hat is saved, Miss Pole!

(*The women, except* MISS MATTY, *crowd around the hat, helping* MISS POLE *to try it on.* MISS MATTY *approaches the* GENTLEMAN.)

MISS MATTY — Excuse me, sir, but was your bank note from Town and County?

(*The* GENTLEMAN *nods.*)

MISS MATTY — And it is worthless?

GENTLEMAN — I had heard there was a chance the bank might break, and apparently it has.

Miss Matty — Thank you.

(*Exit* Gentleman. Mary *goes to* Miss Matty *with some material.*)

Mary — This silk will match the ribbons in your cap.

Miss Matty — Never mind the silks for a few minutes, dear. Town and County is my bank. I think there is some mistake about this, for I am one of the shareholders and I'm sure they would have told me if things had not been going on right. I must return home immediately.

(*Enter* Mrs Barker, *clutching a huge piece of folded grey material.*)

Miss Pole — Good day, Mrs Barker!

Mrs Barker — Thank goodness I have caught you before it grows busy. I require a large amount of grey flannel. It is for my poor dear Bessie. I have been working upon her modesty protector, as I like to call it, but I have run out of material.

(Mrs Barker *holds up the material, her arms extended above her head. It is an enormous pair of bloomers. There is a large hole in the crotch area, which falls exactly level with* Mrs Barker's *head so her face can be seen through the hole.*)

Mrs Barker — I cannot leave it like this or poor Bessie's posterior will be entirely exposed to the elements!

Milliner — I may have a piece large enough in my stores.

(*Exeunt* MRS BARKER *and the* MILLINER.)

JESSIE (*laughing*) Poor Mrs Barker!

MISS POLE Poor Mrs Barker nothing. I would not miss this for anything.

MARY I thought you had no interest in anything today?

MISS POLE That was before there was an unfinished flannel bloomer on the loose!

(*Exeunt* MISS POLE, *followed by* JESSIE.)

MISS MATTY If it is true, I shall only have thirteen pounds a year left. I hope it's not wrong – not wicked – but I am so glad poor Deborah is spared this. She could not have borne to come down in the world. She had such a noble, lofty spirit.

(*Exeunt* MISS MATTY *and* MARY.)

Scene Two

Exterior. The garden at MISS MATTY'S. *Day.*

Enter MARY, MRS JAMIESON, MISS POLE *and* JESSIE.

MRS JAMIESON I hope there is good reason you have summoned us here at such short notice, Miss Smith. You do realise I have had to cancel my afternoon walk with Carlo?

JESSIE With Carlo?

MRS JAMIESON His body may be gone but his spirit roams free.

MISS POLE Where is Miss Matty?

MARY She is running some errands in the village.

MISS POLE What purpose could you have to exclude her?

MARY I do not like to take advantage of her absence, but there is something I must tell you secretly. I hope you will not think it a breach of confidence.

JESSIE What is wrong?

MARY I am telling you because you are dear friends to Miss Matty. She is bankrupt. She has lost everything. She plans to take a single room and keep only the furniture necessary to fill it up.

MRS JAMIESON But that will be hardly anything!

MISS POLE Miss Smith, you were right to tell us. We, the ladies of Cranford here assembled, can resolve something. I imagine we are none of us what may be called rich, though we all possess enough for tastes that are elegant and refined. But we shall all give what we can to assist her. In consideration of the feelings of delicate independence existing in the mind of every refined female, we must contribute in a concealed manner.

JESSIE How will we give our offerings to her then?

MISS POLE Miss Smith, you have a fair hand for forgery. You may write a note from the manager of the bank, informing Miss Matty the amount is the recovered remainder of her shares. Fetch some pens and paper.

(*Exit* MARY. MISS POLE *starts taking off her bonnet.*)

MISS POLE We must each write down the sum we may give and submit it secretly.

(*Enter* MARY *with pens and paper, which she hands round. The women write down the amounts they can give.* MISS POLE *peers at* MRS JAMIESON'S *slip.*)

MISS POLE Mrs Jamieson! You may afford much more than that!

MRS JAMIESON I thought it was to be secret!

MISS POLE Miss Matty has been very kind to you over the years.

MRS JAMIESON Very well. I suppose I could stretch the amount a little.

JESSIE I wish I could give more.

MARY We all love her, and I think we are all better when she is near us. Do not be ashamed, Jessie. Anything you can give will be appreciated.

(*The women fold their slips of paper and put them in* MISS POLE'S *bonnet.*)

MISS POLE Mary, I trust you can add up the amounts and compose the letter?

MARY I shall start work on it straight away. But Miss Matty shall be home soon.

MRS JAMIESON Then we must disappear or she will suspect a mutiny!

(*From offstage, the sudden sound of a huge crash, a man shouting in pain, a horse neighing.*)

MISS POLE It seems we are not the mutineers! Come, we must investigate!

JESSIE Do you think it is safe?

MISS POLE It is not a question of whether it is safe or not. It is our community duty!

(*Exeunt.*)

Scene Three

Exterior. Cranford Village Green. Day.

Enter TWO GENTLEMEN, *carrying* SIGNOR BRUNONI. *His leg is injured and he is crying out in pain. He no longer wears his magician's outfit. Enter* MISS MATTY, *carrying a basket of supplies.*

GENTLEMAN 1 (*to* MISS MATTY) Excuse me, ma'am – is there a surgeon in town?

MISS MATTY Yes, Dr Hoggins. His practice is next door to the general store.

(*The* GENTLEMEN *put* SIGNOR BRUNONI *down. Exit* GENTLEMAN 2.)

MISS MATTY What happened?

GENTLEMAN 1 Our cart lost a wheel on the road out of the village. My master is badly injured.

(*Enter* MISS POLE, MRS JAMIESON, JESSIE *and* MARY.)

MISS MATTY Oh! Have I missed a meeting?

MISS POLE No!

MISS MATTY But you are all together!

MISS POLE No we are not! Mrs Jamieson, fancy meeting you here.

MARY Miss Pole, we must confess.

MISS POLE Miss Smith, control yourself!

MARY Miss Matty, we – we wanted to – surprise you when you returned!

MISS MATTY How lovely! For a moment there I almost thought I had fallen out of favour with my friends. But first we must tend to this poor man. Sir?

(SIGNOR BRUNONI *raises his head for the first time and the women recognize him.*)

JESSIE Signor Brunoni!

MRS JAMIESON Aha! Comeuppance!

(MARY *starts towards him.*)

MRS JAMIESON Stay away from that odious man!

MARY But his leg!

MISS MATTY Mrs Jamieson, we cannot do nothing.

MRS JAMIESON I shall not be party to anything!

(MRS JAMIESON *turns to go.*)

SIGNOR BRUN. (*without an accent*) Madam, please!

MRS JAMIESON I am afraid that the repression of your natural accent is not enough to recommend yourself to me, signor. I have no patience with actors.

SIGNOR BRUN. This is no act, madam, I assure you. I am as Turkish as a pork pie. My name is Samuel Brown. Not Signor Brunoni.

MISS POLE I knew he was not a real magician.

SIGNOR BRUN. My tricks were genuine, I assure you.

MISS MATTY Mr Brown, there is no excuse for what you have done. You have taken money under false pretences.

SIGNOR BRUN. You are right. But it was only the worst of hardships that forced me to do it. My family are in London – my wife, and little Lottie and James too. After the closure of the tanners, I had to leave them to seek some fortune the only way I could. I have not seen them for five months. I have been travelling the country, sending money home whenever I can.

JESSIE You must miss your wife so much.

SIGNOR BRUN. I cannot think of it. It pains me too much.

MRS JAMIESON More than your leg?

SIGNOR BRUN. Much more.

(*Enter* GENTLEMAN 2).

GENTLEMAN 2 The doctor'll see him.

(*The* TWO GENTLEMEN *help* SIGNOR BRUNONI *up.*)

SIGNOR BRUN. Ladies, I hope you can find it in your hearts to forgive me. (*To* MRS JAMIESON.) If there were any way I could bring little Carlos back to you, I would do it.

MRS JAMIESON Carlo! But I thank you for the sentiment, Mr Brown.

JESSIE That does not sound right. Mr Brown, I should like to always remember you as the signor. I hope you don't mind?

SIGNOR BRUN. It fills my heart with gratitude to be remembered by such fine ladies at all.

MISS MATTY Signor, you shall need somewhere to stay while you recover. Allow me to offer my spare room.

SIGNOR BRUN. I could not impose –

MISS MATTY I insist. Mary and I shall be pleased to have you stay.

SIGNOR BRUN. What a town Cranford is for kindness!

(*Exeunt* SIGNOR BRUNONI *and the* GENTLEMEN. *They support the limping* SIGNOR.)

MISS MATTY Do you think I have made a mistake in inviting him to stay? I am not used to keeping company with a man.

MISS POLE You did quite the right thing. As most of the ladies of good family in Cranford are elderly spinsters, or widows without children, if we do not relax a little, and become less exclusive, by and by we shall have no society at all.

MARY — That is very modern-minded of you, Miss Pole.

MISS POLE — I like to be progressive.

MISS MATTY — But it does not solve my dilemma. If Deborah had been alive she would have known what to do with a gentleman visitor. Must I put razors in his dressing room? I have none! Deborah would have had them. And slippers! What about slippers?

MARY — I am sure he can procure some if he needs them. Come, we will set up his room together.

(*The women start to make their way off.*)

MRS JAMIESON — Do you know, if I were not without my Carlo because of him, I should be quite of a mind to forget I ever had any quarrel with Mr Brown. Quite charming!

JESSIE — (*sotto, to* MARY) Perhaps my father shall be free if Mrs Jamieson is to transfer her affections to the signor!

(*Exeunt.*)

Scene Four

Exterior. The garden at MISS MATTY'S. *Day.*

Enter MISS MATTY, *with a tangled mass of bunting that she starts to untangle.*

Miss Matty (*to Deborah*) I suppose that at this time of year you shall not be sad to be gone, Deborah dear. You never did like the Midsummer festivities. "Too much frivolity and a distinct lack of decorum".

(*Behind* Miss Matty, *the house window opens and* Martha *appears there, washing the window.* Miss Matty *does not notice* Martha, *who overhears what she says.*)

Miss Matty (*to Deborah*) I am ruined, you know, my dear. The bank has gone under. I am not very extravagant, and when this week's neck of mutton and Martha's wages and the rent are paid, I have not a farthing owing. But poor Martha! I think she'll be sorry to leave me.

(Miss Matty *looks at her St. Christopher.*)

Miss Matty It will break my heart to part with you. But I must offer Martha some bonus before I send her out.

(*She takes the St. Christopher off.* Martha *looks distraught and silently closes the window. Enter* Mary.)

Mary We shall have to order some more tea from Mr Johnson. We have only a few leaves left. Tea really is one of those things that is in constant demand!

Miss Matty Is the signor all right?

Mary He seems quite well. I think he is taking an afternoon doze in the parlour.

MISS MATTY Then I shall take the opportunity to ask Martha to refresh his bed sheets.

(MISS MATTY *hands the bunting to* MARY. *Exit* MISS MATTY. MARY *starts sorting out the bunting. Enter* MARTHA.)

MARTHA Is it true, Miss Mary? Is it true? I'll never leave her! No; I won't. I know when I've got a good missus, and I thought she knew she's got a good servant –

MARY But Martha –

MARTHA Don't "but Martha" me!

MARY Listen to reason –

MARTHA I'll not listen ter reason. Reason always means what someone else has got ter say. Now I'll say what I want ter say, reason or not! I've money in the savings bank and a good stock of clothes and I'm not going ter leave Miss Matty.

MARY I know you would be a great loss to Miss Matty. But she will have so little, so very little, to live upon, that I don't see how she could find you food – she will even be pressed for her own.

MARTHA Was that why she wouldn't order a pudding today? I'll make her a pudding and I'll pay forrit myself – so mind yer see she eats it. Many people have been comforted in their sorrow by seein' a good dish on the table.

(MARTHA *gathers her skirts up and marches off determinedly.*)

(*Exit* MARTHA. MARY *goes back to sorting out the bunting. Enter* MISS MATTY.)

MISS MATTY I don't know where that girl goes sometimes. I suppose the sheets will have to wait, as I fear my footsteps on the stair awoke the signor. His snoring seems to have stopped, anyway.

MISS POLE (*at the top of her voice, from offstage*) Miss Matty!

MARY Well, he shall certainly be awake now.

(*Enter* MISS POLE, *breathless.*)

MISS POLE (*urgently*) Miss Matty! Mary! Quick, you must come! The party from Paris – they have returned!

(*Exeunt, led by* MISS POLE.)

Scene Five

Exterior. Cranford Village Green. Day.

Enter MARY *and* JESSIE.

JESSIE What should I say to him? It seems so long since I last saw him – so much has happened –

MARY Calm yourself. It will be easier when you see him.

JESSIE I hope so. I feel like my heart is going to burst out of my chest with beating.

(*Enter* MISS POLE, MISS MATTY, MRS JAMIESON *and* CAPTAIN BROWN.)

MISS POLE Just because you are younger, I do not think it was very fair of you to rush ahead of us.

MARY You haven't missed anything. The party are still inside the inn.

MRS JAMIESON What are they waiting for?

(MISS POLE *sees* MAJOR GORDON.)

MISS POLE Arrange yourselves, ladies, the major approaches!

(JESSIE *nervously turns to flee as the women arrange themselves in a line.* MARY *grabs her and pulls her back.*)

MARY (*to* JESSIE) He will be pleased to see you.

(JESSIE *darts behind the other women. Enter* MAJOR GORDON.)

CAPT. BROWN Good to see you back, Brown.

(*The two men shake hands.*)

MAJ. GORDON I am happy to be back.

(*He looks down the line of women.*)

MAJ. GORDON Miss Brown could not be here? She is well? I came back – I cut short my trip as soon as I heard about her sister. (*To* CAPTAIN BROWN.) I am so sorry for both of you for your terrible loss.

(MISS POLE *harumphs indignantly.*)

MAJ. GORDON Have I offended you, madam?

MISS POLE — We all know round here precisely why you have come back now.

MAJ. GORDON — You do?

MISS POLE — You see the one remaining obstacle to your union with Miss Jessie Brown has been removed.

MAJ. GORDON — My concern was only for her well-being and that of her family.

MRS JAMIESON — You do not love her any longer?

MAJ. GORDON — I did not realize my emotions were under scrutiny.

MISS POLE — Then you do not understand women very well at all.

MAJ. GORDON — Perhaps I should go. When you see Jessie, tell her I . . . I will always have oranges.

MISS POLE — Oranges!

(MAJOR GORDON *turns to go.* JESSIE *steps out from behind the women.*)

JESSIE — Does that go for apples and pears also, Major Gordon?

(MAJOR GORDON *looks back in surprise.*)

MAJ. GORDON — You have only to ask and they are yours.

JESSIE — That sentiment is true for us both.

(MAJOR GORDON *goes to* JESSIE, *drawing something out of his pocket. He bends onto one knee and brings out a ring box.*)

MAJ. GORDON I have carried this with me in the hope – the prayer – that one day we may be reunited. That our time may come.

(JESSIE *goes onto her knees in front of him.*)

JESSIE It has.

(*She opens the box, takes the ring out and puts it on her finger. She grabs* MAJOR GORDON *and kisses him.*)

MISS POLE Mary, avert your eyes!

MRS JAMIESON Captain Brown, surely you are most outraged?

CAPT. BROWN I gave my consent long ago.

(JESSIE *and* MAJOR GORDON *break apart.*)

JESSIE Father –

CAPT. BROWN You have been a good daughter long enough. Now it is time to be a good wife.

JESSIE I shall endeavour to be both.

(JESSIE *and* CAPTAIN BROWN *embrace.*)

MISS MATTY (*to* MAJOR GORDON) Thomas – Mr Holbrook has not returned from Paris with you?

MAJ. GORDON I'm afraid the last I heard of him, he had gone to Lyon.

(MISS POLE *gasps in horror.*)

MARY What's wrong?

MISS POLE Mr Holbrook is – in Lyon!

MARY (*confused*) I am sure it is pleasant there.

MISS POLE How could it be? It is – Lyon!

MRS JAMIESON I know the French have little to recommend themselves beyond their fashion, but need you be so adverse to them?

MAJ. GORDON (*to* MISS POLE) Have you been to Lyon?

MISS POLE Do I look like I have?

MAJ. GORDON Then you have some other reason for particularly disliking the city?

MISS POLE (*confused*) The city? Excuse me.

(MISS POLE *pulls* MARY *aside.* MISS MATTY *talks quietly to* MAJOR GORDON.)

MISS POLE Lyon is a city?

MARY Yes. In France. Like Paris. What did you think it was?

MISS POLE Well, from the solemnity of Major Gordon's pronouncement, I assumed it was a – a euphemism for saying that Mr Holbrook was – (*She mumbles something inaudible.*)

MARY I'm sorry?

(MISS POLE *mumbles again.*)

MARY What?

MISS POLE In heaven!

MARY — You thought he was dead? Oh, Miss Pole –

MISS POLE — Do not feel sorry for me! It is an easy mistake to make. French is a most morbid language, anything they say could be to do with death.

MAJ. GORDON — I am sorry I do not bring gladder news of Mr Holbrook.

MISS MATTY — You have brought great happiness to us all.

CAPT. BROWN — Come – you must all come to the house for cake!

(*Exeunt* CAPTAIN BROWN, MAJOR GORDON, JESSIE, MARY *and* MRS JAMIESON.)

MISS POLE — Will the man never learn? Cake is not at all suitable to be served at an engagement celebration!

(*Exeunt* MISS MATTY *and* MISS POLE.)

Scene Six

Exterior. The garden at MISS MATTY'S. *Day.*

Enter MISS MATTY, MARY, MRS JAMIESON *and* MISS POLE. *They arrange each other's floral headdresses for the party.*

MARY — It is a wonderful thing to be engaged. And for Jessie to be crowned the Midsummer Queen too!

MISS MATTY — It was only fitting.

MISS POLE — I am most thankful I have never been married.

MISS MATTY Marriage is a risk, to be sure, but I can remember the time when I looked forward to being married as much as any girl.

MARY To who?

MISS MATTY Not to any particular person. Only the old story, you know, of ladies saying, "When I marry", and gentlemen, "If I marry".

MARY (*to* MISS MATTY) Does it ever sadden you, that you did not marry?

MISS MATTY Perhaps there have been times when I have felt a yearning in my heart when I see a mother with her baby in her arms. I fancy it may be a very happy state.

MARY I am sure it is, but I doubt I shall have occasion to experience it.

MISS MATTY Do not be frightened by Miss Pole from being married. (*She finishes* MARY'S *headdress.*) There.

MRS JAMIESON We must be on our way. I do not want to be late!

MISS MATTY You two go on ahead. Mary will make me presentable.

(*Exeunt* MISS POLE *and* MRS JAMIESON.)

MARY Shall I pin your headdress for you?

MISS MATTY I think – I think I should rather leave my cap on.

MARY Why did you take up wearing that cap, Miss Matty?

MISS MATTY — When – when Mr Holbrook left, I suppose I considered myself from that point on, quite a widow.

(*Enter* MARTHA, *dragging* JEM *behind her.*)

MARTHA — Please, ma'am, he's only Jem Hearn, but he wants ter marry me. And please, ma'am, we want ter take a lodger – just one quiet lodger, to make ends meet. Miss Matty, if I may be so bold, would you have any objection to lodging with us? Jem wants it as much as I do! (*To* JEM.) Yer great oaf, why can't yer back me up? (*To* MISS MATTY.) He does want it, very bad, only yer see, he's dazed at bein' called ter speak before ladies of quality.

JEM — It's not that. It's that yer've taken me all of a sudden and I didn't think ter get married so soon and quick words does flabbergast a man. (*To* MISS MATTY.) It's not that I'm against it, ma'am, only Martha has such quick ways once she gets a thing into her head, and marriage – marriage nails a man. But I dare say I shan't mind it after it's over.

MARTHA — Don't mind him, he'll come to. He's only taken aback with the suddenness of the joy.

JEM — Ay! If Miss Matty weren't ter lodge with us I've no mind ter be cumbered with strange folk in the house.

MISS MATTY — Marriage is a very solemn thing, Martha.

JEM — It is indeed. Not that I've no objections ter Martha.

MARTHA Now yer shamin' me before my missus and all!

JEM Nay, Martha, don't cry! A man only likes ter have breathin' time.

(JEM *tries to grab* MARTHA'S *hand but she pulls away.*)

JEM (*to* MISS MATTY) I hope, ma'am, that yer know I am bound ter respect anyone who has been kind ter Martha. E'er since I met her, I looked on her ter be my wife at some time, and she has often spoken of yer as the kindest lady there e'er was and though the plain truth is I wouldn't like ter be troubled with lodgers of the commonest sort, if yer'd honour us by livin' with us, I'm sure Martha would do her best ter make yer comfortable and I'd keep outta yer way as much as I could which I reckon'd be the best kindness an awkward chap like me could do.

MISS MATTY Pray, don't let any thought of me hurry you into marriage!

MARY But Miss Matilda will think of your plan, and she shall never forget your kindness.

JEM (*to* MISS MATTY) Don't yer worry, ma'am, I'm willing enough for marriage and give me time ter get accustomed and I'll have no complaint. (*To* MARTHA.) So what's the use of crying so, and slapping me when I come near?

(MARTHA *flounces off angrily, followed by* JEM. *Exeunt* MARTHA *and* JEM.)

MARY Another engagement!

MISS MATTY Why don't you go and tell the ladies?

MARY Won't you come?

MISS MATTY I shall catch you up. Go on.

(*Exit* MARY. MISS MATTY *pulls a letter out.*)

MISS MATTY (*to Deborah*) I had a letter yesterday. From the manager of the bank, confirming I have lost everything. It is absolute now I have it in writing, I suppose.

(*Enter* THOMAS HOLBROOK, *unseen by* MISS MATTY. THOMAS *knocks.*)

MISS MATTY Just a moment! I'm coming!

(MISS MATTY *tucks the letter away and adjusts her cap. She turns, and stops short as she sees* THOMAS.)

MISS MATTY Mr Holbrook!

THOMAS Miss Jenkyns.

MISS MATTY I understood you were in Lyon.

THOMAS I was.

MISS MATTY It did not please you?

THOMAS It was not how I thought it would be. Something was missing in every street, every monument, every person I saw.

(*Their eyes meet for a moment, then* MR HOLBROOK *delves into his travelling bag.*)

THOMAS I brought something back for you. I saw it and – thought of you.

(THOMAS *holds out a turban.* MISS MATTY *laughs.*)

THOMAS If it is not right, I can – well, I cannot return it, I suppose, but I am sure I could find some use for it.

MISS MATTY No – it is perfect. Thank you.

(*She takes the turban.*)

THOMAS Are you joining the party out on the village green? Perhaps I might accompany you?

(*He offers his arm.*)

MISS MATTY One moment.

(MISS MATTY *unties her cap and takes it off. She struggles to put on the turban.* THOMAS *helps her, then offers her his arm again. She takes it. Exeunt.*)

Scene Seven

Exterior. Cranford Village Green. Day.

Enter MISS POLE, MRS JAMIESON, MARY, MARTHA *and* JEM. MARY *and* MISS POLE *help* MARTHA *and* JEM *to string up bunting.*

MISS POLE We must be ready to present the letter to Miss Matty when she arrives. And remember, we do not know what is within! It shall be up to her if she wishes to tell us.

JEM She's coming! And a man with her and all!

(Miss Pole, Mary *and* Mrs Jamieson *rush to look.*)

Mary — Mr Holbrook!

Mrs Jamieson — He is not in Lyon after all!

Miss Pole — Quickly, before Miss Matty sees! And remember – be discrete.

(*Enter* Miss Matty *and* Thomas.)

Miss Pole — (*waving the letter in excitement*) Miss Matty, a letter has arrived for you!

(Miss Matty *takes the letter.*)

Miss Matty — The post does not usually come on a Sunday.

Mary — It was a special delivery!

(Miss Matty *opens the letter and reads.*)

Mary — It is nice to see you back in Cranford, Mr Holbrook.

Thomas — It is most pleasant to me too.

Miss Matty — Mary, I don't understand what is writ in this letter. It is from the bank, saying some of my funds have been recovered. But I received this letter – (*She pulls out the real letter.*) – just yesterday, confirming all was lost. I shall have to contact them immediately.

(Miss Matty *turns to go.*)

Miss Pole — No! I mean, that is to say . . . oh, Miss Matty, forgive us!

MISS MATTY For what?

MISS POLE We are responsible for this letter. It is all lies!

MISS MATTY There is no money?

MARY There is money. But not from the bank. Miss Matty, it broke our heart to see you so bereft, so we took it upon ourselves to each make a small contribution.

MISS MATTY I cannot accept that –

MISS POLE It is no disgrace to accept generosity from friends!

MISS MATTY Do you know, I have been thinking for a long while now about what new course my life may now take.

MRS JAMIESON You cannot be thinking of moving away!

MISS MATTY No. I do not think I would ever leave Cranford. But I have made a decision. I am going to open a teashop.

MISS POLE You are to become a shopkeeper?

MISS MATTY And Martha, Jem – I should like you both to live with me. It really is high time there was a man about the house.

MARTHA We'd be honoured, ma'am. Wouldn't we?

JEM Ay, honoured.

MARY Congratulations, Miss Matty – sorry, Miss Matilda.

MISS MATTY — Do you know, I think I should like to be known as I always have been. As Miss Matty.

MRS JAMIESON — Bravo indeed!

(*Enter* MAJOR GORDON. *He is holding a French poodle in his arms.*)

MRS JAMIESON — Major Gordon! What have you got there?

MAJ. GORDON — I purchased this fellow in Paris, but now I find myself quite unable to find houseroom for him.

MRS JAMIESON — He is a beautiful specimen.

MAJ. GORDON — If you are enamoured of him, perhaps you might desire to provide him with a good home?

MRS JAMIESON — Major, I should be delighted!

(MAJOR GORDON *gives the poodle to* MRS JAMIESON.)

MRS JAMIESON — (*to the dog*) You and Carlo would have got on famously, wouldn't you my little poochy whoochy?

MARY — (*sotto, to* MAJOR GORDON) That was awfully good timing, Major.

MAJ. GORDON — (*sotto*) I must confess it was a scheme devised by Jessie. To give her father some small respite from Mrs Jamieson's constant attentions.

MARY — It seems to have done the trick.

(MRS JAMIESON *is making kissy noises at the poodle.*)

MARTHA Quick! Miss Brown is coming!

(*The women rush over to greet her. Enter* JESSIE, *in her outfit as Midsummer Queen.*)

(MAJOR GORDON *joins her. The women shower them with flower petals and* MAJOR GORDON *places a floral crown on* JESSIE'S *head. The Midsummer party begins, with singing and dancing.* MARTHA *and* JEM *kiss alongside* JESSIE *and* MAJOR GORDON. MISS MATTY *allows* THOMAS *to give her a peck on a cheek. Exeunt, the celebrations in full swing.*)